BIRMINGHAM
TRANSPORT

MIKE HITCHES

SUTTON PUBLISHING LIMITED

Sutton Publishing Limited
Phoenix Mill · Thrupp · Stroud
Gloucestershire · GL5 2BU

First published 1999

British Library Cataloguing in Publication Data
A catalogue record for this book is available from the
British Library.

ISBN 0-7509-1670-2

Typeset in 10/12 Perpetua.
Typesetting and origination by
Sutton Publishing Limited.
Printed in Great Britain by
Ebenezer Baylis, Worcester.

Dedicated to the memory of my late parents, Winifred and Howard Hitches, both of whom were born and bred in Birmingham and were true Brummies.

CONTENTS

INTRODUCTION

Birmingham has long been a centre of manufacture. Indeed, in the early eighteenth century the town was producing tanned goods and cloth. The Industrial Revolution was already showing its effects by this time, with the thriving South Staffordshire coalfields producing coal just north of the town and Black Country sandstone quarries providing coarse stones for the edge tool industry. Pig iron from the Cannock area was also finding a growing market in Birmingham by then. As the eighteenth century developed, Birmingham was expanding into gun manufacture, along with brass buttons, toys and other brass articles. Fashions also brought a market for shoe buckles to Birmingham and the town became known for its high-quality jewellery. There were firms who went into enamelling, japanning and papier mâché products. Antique programmes on television today often remark on the high standard of the papier mâché trays and table tops that were made in Birmingham.

By the first half of the nineteenth century guns, jewellery, buttons and brass products had become staple Birmingham industries, with new products, such as pearl-covered buttons, naval brass, plumbing, cabinet fittings, wire, lamps, carriage fittings and brass bedsteads constantly being introduced. The town then branched out into locomotive tube products, hinges, fire irons, fenders, grates, wood screws and steel pens. Towards the end of the century the chocolate works at Bournville was established, and as the new century dawned the thriving city, gaining its Royal Charter in 1889, became a centre for the manufacture of bicycles, motorcycles, cars and electrical goods.

With such a diversity of products being turned out from Birmingham's workshops and factories, transport was essential to its economy. Until James Brindley opened the Birmingham Canal in 1768, the town relied on packhorses for the transit of its products. The following year the canal network was extended and Birmingham was linked to the Thames, Trent, Humber, Mersey and Severn rivers, allowing the faster movement of finished goods and raw materials, the town becoming a hub of the canal system.

Birmingham was also to become the hub of a new form of transport – the railways. In 1837 the Grand Junction Railway was opened, to be followed a year later by the London and Birmingham Railway, and the two companies met at the town. Ironically, Birmingham businessmen showed no interest in the establishment of the railways and it was Liverpool investment that paid for their construction. However, the new railways linked Birmingham with Manchester, Liverpool and London, and it was not long before other new railway companies became interested in establishing routes into the rapidly expanding industrial town to take advantage of potential goods traffic. The Birmingham and Gloucester Railway entered Birmingham in 1840 and the Great Western Railway line from Oxford was established in 1845. By the early 1850s the town had two important railway stations at New Street and Snow Hill.

As the town, and later city, continued to expand and the population increased, public street transport was developed. Horse buses plied their trade as the nineteenth century drew to a close but trams and motor buses made their appearance as the twentieth century dawned. Two important providers of public street transport emerged in 1904, Birmingham City Transport (operated by the city corporation) and the privately owned Birmingham and Midland Motor Omnibus Company (affectionately known as the Midland Red). Birmingham City Transport developed the electric tramway network and operated motor buses, while the Midland Red ran motor buses that connected Birmingham with other Midland towns and cities.

The city, however, is best known for its motorcycle and car products, the manufacturers of which were to become household names. Companies like BSA, Velocette and Ariel turned out motorcycles by the thousand until Japanese competition put them out of business in the 1960s. The Austin motor works at Longbridge began producing motor cars in 1905, many of its vehicles becoming world famous.

The city also turned out commercial vehicles, at Morris Commercial, and lorries and buses were bodied in Birmingham by Metropolitan-Cammell. This firm was also known for turning out railway wagons, coaches and even whole trains. The London underground trains are built by the Metropolitan-Cammell company and modern Sprinter trains have Metropolitan-Cammell bodies.

As if to highlight Birmingham's role in road transport, the city is now also the hub of the motorway network, owing to three motorways, the M1, M5 and M6, all meeting in the city at the Gravelly Hill Interchange, more famously, and humorously, known as Spaghetti Junction. Thus Birmingham has been the hub of the three most important transport networks, the canals, the railways and the roads, all of which go to highlight the importance of Birmingham as a manufacturing centre and Britain's second city.

LNWR 2–2–2–0 compound no. 311 *Rich Francis Roberts* waits at New Street station in 1903, an example of the nineteenth-century locos which operated on LNWR train services between Birmingham and London Euston.

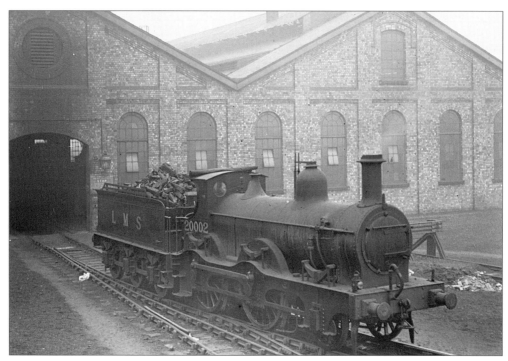

Ex-Midland Railway 'Kirtley' 2–4–0 no. 20002 outside Bournville locoshed in 1935. The MR also operated express trains out of New Street to Bristol, and these engines were a familiar sight on such trains in the latter years of the nineteenth century.

CHAPTER ONE

THE CANALS

Birmingham was a rapidly expanding industrial town by the early eighteenth century but development was hampered by poor road systems. Any raw materials or finished goods were transported by packhorse or horse and cart, which meant that only small quantities could be carried at a high cost. Raw materials such as iron and coal were brought from the Black Country, the mines and ironworks being situated in the area between Birmingham and Wolverhampton. In order to improve transport between these two important towns and to connect with canals from the north, such as the Trent and Mersey Canal, an advertisement was placed in *Aris's Gazette* on 26 January 1767 to consider the possibility of cutting a canal from Wolverhampton to Birmingham, via the coal-mining areas in the Black Country. This meeting led to the establishment of the Birmingham Canal Navigation Company and a route was surveyed by the great canal-builder James Brindley. A bill for construction was presented to Parliament which received Royal Assent on 24 February 1768. The canal had a rather circuitous route when opened on 21 September 1772 but its effects were immediately felt. The price of coal transport fell by half overnight and this short-lived transport revolution was underway. The BCN was not averse to becoming involved with other canal companies, however, and an acrimonious dispute arose with the promoters of the Birmingham and Fazeley Canal Company, which was only resolved when the two companies merged in 1784. This canal was finally opened in 1789, with a branch to Digbeth opening ten years later. Another canal that joined the BCN in Birmingham included the Warwick and Birmingham, which joined at Digbeth, and provided the BCN with a direct link to London. The BCN would charge high tolls to competing operators at its junctions, which would allow the later railway companies to steal canal trade as they could undercut canal prices and were able to move freight much more quickly than the canal companies. It could be argued that the BCN saw the competition coming and employed Thomas Telford to shorten its main route, work which was completed between 1827 and 1838. The latter date was when the London and Birmingham Railway opened and made a junction with the Grand Junction Railway, itself opened a year earlier, whose line ran through the Black Country.

Another important canal that ran into Birmingham was the Worcester and Birmingham Canal. This was constructed under an act of 1791. The canal officially started at Worcester Bar, near Broad Street, because the BCN would not allow access to its own route without payment of their high tolls. The Worcester company refused to pay these tolls, so a stop (the Bar) was placed on them and all goods carried on the Worcester and Birmingham Canal which were for destinations north of the bar had to be transferred from their boats to those of the BCN, which slowed up traffic considerably.

With such squabbling continuing between the canal companies, the new railway companies took their chance and easily took away canal trade. Many of the railway routes into Birmingham run parallel with the canals; for example, the Midland line between New Street and King's Norton runs alongside the Worcester and Birmingham Canal as far as Bournville, and the LNWR Stour Valley line runs next to the BCN between Wolverhampton and Birmingham.

The canals survived as transport carriers until after the Second World War but trade diminished following the growth of the railways. Today, they are mostly pleasure craft routes and the city of Birmingham has done much to restore banks and towpaths, making these eighteenth-century engineering marvels attractive for boating and walkers alike. This thereby ensures a future for this transport network that allowed Birmingham to grow so rapidly.

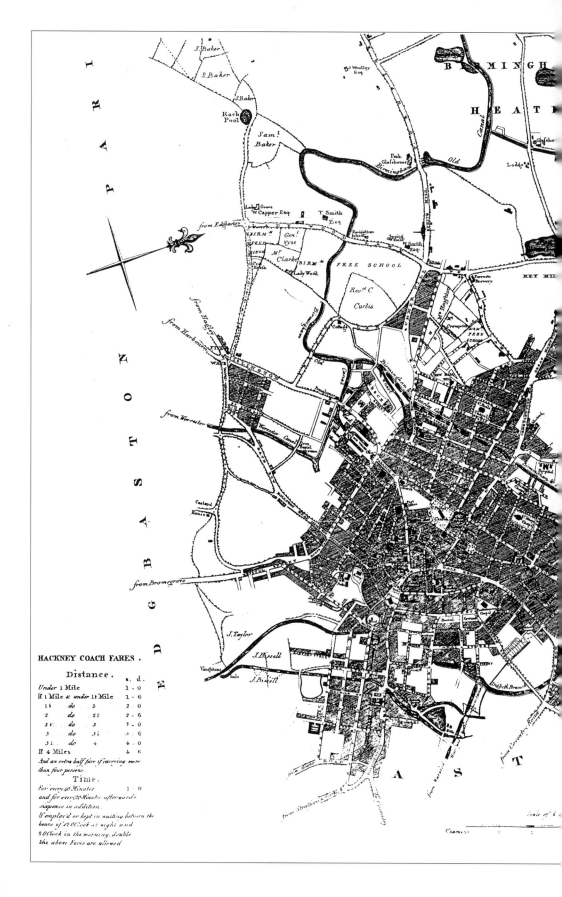

HACKNEY COACH FARES.

Distance.

		s.	d.
Under 1 Mile		1	0
If 1 Mile & under 1½ Mile		1	6
1½	do 2	2	0
2	do 2½	2	6
2½	do 3	3	0
3	do 3½	3	6
3½	do 4	4	0
If 4 Miles		4	6

And an extra half fare if carrying more
than four persons.

Time.

	s.	d.
For every 40 Minutes	1	0

and for every 20 Minutes afterwards
sixpence in addition.

If employ'd or kept in waiting between the
hours of 12 O'Clock at night and
3 O'Clock in the morning, double
the above Fares are allowed

8

A map of Birmingham in 1810, twenty-seven years before the first railway, the Grand Junction, entered the town. The map shows the canal system that served the town and permitted its rapid growth into a major industrial centre. Within a century this small town grew to become Britain's second city, and was called 'the city of a thousand trades'. On the map are the Worcester and Birmingham Canal, Birmingham Canal Navigation routes, the Birmingham Old Canal, the Birmingham and Fazeley Canal with its Digbeth branch, and the Warwick and Birmingham Canal. Such was the development of the canal system in the eighteenth and early nineteenth centuries that Birmingham is reputed to have more miles of canal than Venice, although some sections are not as picturesque as their Italian counterparts. The city of Birmingham has done much to improve the canals within the city boundary, however, and several stretches are very attractive and a definite tourist asset.

Birmingham Canal with Winson Green Road crossing in the foreground and Lea Bridge in the background. In this 1956 view the canal has no traffic but the towpaths appear to be well maintained.

Birmingham Canal navigations at Smethwick. Here there is a split bridge situated at Spon Lane top lock.

Sandwell Colliery coal staiths at Smethwick. This view shows the arches of Summit Bridge and a railway bridge. The transport of coal brought much revenue to the Birmingham Canal Navigations and several boating companies carried freight along this canal network. These included Thomas Clayton of Oldbury, T. & S. Element Ltd, Ernie Thomas of Walsall and Samuel Barlow's of Birmingham, the latter company only operating on the BCN for a few years.

The remains of the pumping house on the BCN between the Birmingham and Wolverhampton levels at Smethwick.

Thomas Telford's Galton Bridge at Smethwick's Roebuck Lane. The bridge spans the engineer's shorter BCN route to Wolverhampton and was constructed in 1829 at Horseley Ironworks. It remains a tribute to Telford's abilities as a civil engineer as it spans 150 feet. The bridge is now obscured by a new dual carriageway road that crosses the canal at this point.

The Stewart aqueduct at Smethwick which carries Brindley's old canal route above the new Telford line; this crosses at right angles below.

The BCN Birmingham and Fazeley Canal's Digbeth branch passing under the London and Birmingham Railway at Proof House Junction in 1958. The junction is so named because the Birmingham Gun Proofing House is situated above at this point. The city was famous as a manufacturer of guns for over a century, and rifles used by the Confederate Army during the American Civil War were supplied by Birmingham manufacturers.

Another view of the Digbeth branch near Proof House Junction. The railway bridge above, with a train passing over it, still retains its original stonework arch.

Birmingham and Warwick Junction Canal at Sandy Lane Bridge, Bordesley, in 1960. This waterway became part of the Grand Union Canal when it was formed in 1929 to provide a complete link between Birmingham and London. The Great Western Railway line between Snow Hill, Moor Street and Paddington crosses the canal here.

The Birmingham and Warwick Junction Canal passing below the railway spur from the Midland Railway's Camp Hill line to Proof House Junction. From here the railway gains access to New Street station. The canal itself was opened as late as 1844 and was forced to compete with the railways from the outset.

The Garrison Lane locks at Brickyard Crossing on the Birmingham and Warwick Junction Canal. The canal connects Warwick Bar, Digbeth, with Salford Bridge, situated below the Gravelly Hill Interchange (Spaghetti Junction). Two important railway routes also pass at this point. In the distance is the London and Birmingham main line between New Street and London (Euston) and in the foreground is the Midland Railway's Saltley to Camp Hill line. In the background is the Morris Commercial vehicle factory at Adderley Park. This company was a manufacturer of commercial vehicles, including small vans and lorries. In the slump years of the 1980s the company had financial problems and was taken over by Daf Trucks, a Dutch commercial vehicle company. They abandoned the works a few years later and it was bought out by the firm who still produced small vans on the site, now trading as LDV. This venture appears to have been successful and the future of the works seems assured.

The starting point of the Worcester and Birmingham Canal at Gas Street Basin, looking towards Broad Street tunnel. The Worcester Bar, where this canal met the Birmingham Navigations canal system, is just beyond this point. Goods were transferred between the boats of the two companies because the Worcester and Birmingham company would not pay the high tolls demanded by the BCN. Today Gas Street Basin is a starting point for cruises along the Worcester and Birmingham canal system, with 'Riverboat Shuffles' – pleasure boats with bands aboard – operating over part of the route. The Basin itself is now a leisure area and a public house is on the site.

Broad Street tunnel, looking towards the Worcester and Birmingham Canal at James Bridge Junction. The Worcester and Birmingham Canal is 30 miles long and contains fifty-eight locks, the longest flight being at Tardebigge between Alvechurch and Droitwich. There are also five tunnels, at Edgbaston, King's Norton (this being just beyond the junction with the Stratford-on-Avon Canal), Shortwood, Tardebigge and Dunhampstead.

The aqueduct at Holliday Street, *c.* 1960. This structure was built by the Midland Railway to carry the Worcester and Birmingham Canal because it had to be moved when the railway company extended its Birmingham West Suburban Railway from its original starting point in Granville Street to New Street station. Work on this extension commenced in 1883 and was completed in 1885, the line actually running alongside the canal until just beyond Bournville. This arrangement emphasized the influence that the railway had on canal traffic, in much the same way motorways in close proximity to railways highlight the takeover by roads since the 1960s.

The Worcester and Birmingham Canal next to the BWSR at the site of Church Road station. A northbound express train, headed by a 'Peak' diesel-electric loco, is passing through the northbound railway tunnel on its way to New Street station.

The Worcester and Birmingham Canal alongside the Midland Railway's Birmingham West Suburban Railway at the site of Church Road station, 1970. The entrance to the canal's Edgbaston tunnel is visible on the left.

The Worcester and Birmingham Canal at Bournville, showing Cadbury's chocolate warehouse, known as 'Waterside', and the company's own loco, no. 10, an 0–4–0 saddle tank built by Pecketts of Bristol in 1955.

Cadbury Brothers' Waterside warehouse on the bank of the Worcester and Birmingham canal. The warehouse was situated on the opposite bank to Bournville station and the chocolate factory. The works were established on a greenfield site near to Bournbrook in 1879 to enable a move from their premises in the centre of Birmingham. The factory needed a constant supply of clean water and their establishment in the centre of town was inadequate for their requirements. It was Cadbury who coined the name 'Bournville' because it sounded French and France had a reputation for producing fine quality chocolate. Their decision to move to the area was no doubt influenced by the existence of the canal and the recently opened Midland Railway's Birmingham West Suburban Railway. The company used both systems to transport raw materials and finished products. In this view boats belonging to the Severn and Canal Carrying Company, in which the Worcester and Birmingham canal company had an interest, can be seen close to the warehouse. The canal continued to be used by Cadbury's until the early 1960s and chocolate crumb was brought from Gloucester by Charlie Atkins, known as 'Chocolate Charlie', in his boat *Mendip* until 1961. Children of the boat operators were always treated to chocolate by Cadbury's, which they no doubt missed when boat trade ceased. Cadbury's established their own railway system at Bournville in 1884 to transport goods within the works and to connect with the Waterside warehouse. They even had their own mainline wagons, some of which can be seen here, that were loaded at the warehouse. The company's railway was closed in May 1976 after freight transport was shifted from rail and canal to the roads, the Waterside warehouse also closing at the same time.

Since the demise of canal goods traffic the Worcester and Birmingham canal has been used for leisure purposes as much of its route runs through attractive rural country. It also connects with the River Severn at Worcester, itself a popular tourist spot. Here, a pleasure boat passes Bournville on its way to Birmingham in 1990.

The 2,726-yard King's Norton tunnel on the Worcester and Birmingham Canal at the Hopwood end, close to Alvechurch, in the 1950s. The tunnel was also known variously as 'Wast Hills tunnel' or 'Westhill tunnel'.

King's Norton tunnel recedes into the background as the canal makes its way towards Alvechurch, an attractive village just outside the Birmingham boundary and midway to Redditch. This used to be a town famous in its time for needle manufacture. The industry has now disappeared.

The Worcester and Birmingham Canal near Alvechurch. The setting here is very rural and it is difficult to imagine that the city of Birmingham is not far away.

Inside the 613-yard Shortwood tunnel, between Alvechurch and Tardebigge, 1950s.

The rural setting of Shortwood tunnel on the Worcester and Birmingham Canal. From here the canal runs on to Diglis Basin, Worcester, where it joins the River Severn.

CHAPTER TWO

THE RAILWAYS

Birmingham became part of the infant railway network with the opening of the Grand Junction Railway in 1837. Its line ran from Warrington, Cheshire, where it connected with the Liverpool and Manchester Railway, which had been operating since 1829, to a station at Vauxhall in Birmingham. Only a year later the London and Birmingham Railway also began operations from Euston Square, London, to Curzon Street, Birmingham, making the West Midlands town a hub between the cotton centre of Manchester, the major seaport at Liverpool and London. The new railways allowed the town of Birmingham to expand even more rapidly. Interestingly, however, both railways were built with financial backing from Liverpool; Birmingham businessmen showed little or no interest in either scheme. They felt that it was unnecessary for them to be involved because they were not concerned with the transport of their products, as they were sold at 'the factory gate', and it was up to the purchaser to arrange his own transport. As far as raw materials were concerned, the canals served all of their needs. Despite this lack of interest, Birmingham benefited greatly when the new railways became established and goods were soon transferred to them from the canals. The railways could offer faster transport times than those offered by the canal companies, and they could also beat their prices. Canal companies suffered as a result and many went into decline, as did stagecoach companies, who lost passengers to the faster railways.

Such was the lure of potential traffic as industrial Birmingham continued its expansion that it was no surprise when other railway companies began to develop lines that would enter the town, and this set up often fierce competition for both freight and passengers. In 1840 the Birmingham and Gloucester Railway was opened as far as Cheltenham, via the steep Lickey Bank gradient, from a temporary Birmingham terminus at Camp Hill. This line met the Bristol and Gloucester Railway and was taken over by the Midland Railway in the mid-1840s from right under the nose of the broad gauge Great Western Railway, who had been keen to obtain this route to Birmingham from its own heartland at Bristol. The Midland also took control of the Birmingham West Suburban Railway in 1875, developing it into an express route from New Street station, which was opened by the London and North Western Railway in 1854. The LNWR was formed in 1846 with the GJR and L&B soon amalgamated into it. The LNWR showed their gratitude to the Midland for keeping out the broad gauge GWR by allowing the Derby company access to the new station. The station was subsequently extended in 1880 to accommodate the Midland more comfortably.

The last company to reach Birmingham was the Great Western Railway. The GWR took control of the Birmingham and Oxford Junction Railway in 1848, the line opening in 1852. This was after the company had been embroiled in nasty disputes with the LNWR, who tried every trick it could to prevent its broad gauge rival reaching Birmingham and competing with the Euston company for traffic between the West Midlands town and London. The GWR route terminated at a modest wooden station called Snow Hill which was improved in 1871 and again in 1906 to become the most affectionately remembered structure of all. The GWR had control of a branch that ran to Stratford-upon-Avon, via Shirley and Henley-in-Arden, which opened in 1908, providing much suburban traffic that went on to terminate at Moor Street station, opened in 1909. The LNWR also had its own branches, to Harborne and Lichfield, providing Birmingham with a substantial rail network. However, like the canals before them, the railways in Birmingham almost succumbed to the greater flexibility of road transport (much of which was built in Birmingham) until the 1980s and 1990s, when excess traffic attracted the Birmingham population back to the trains, just in time to ensure their future.

On 16 July 1920 two LNWR locomotives, 'Jumbo' class 2–4–0 no. 514 *Puck* and 'Precursor' class 4–4–0 no. 218 *Daphne* wait under the arched roof of Birmingham New Street station with their respective passenger trains. New Street station was opened on 1 June 1854 and took seven years to construct at a cost of £500,000. The L&B and GJR had been using Curzon Street, with its famous Doric arch (now preserved), since 1839. Vauxhall station on the GJR was then relegated to the role of goods depot and eventually demolished. When the two companies became part of the mighty London and North Western Railway in 1846, Curzon Street was considered to be too far away from the centre of Birmingham and plans were drawn up for a new station, to be called Navigation Street, closer to the centre. The station was never called Navigation Street: it was called New Street when it was opened. The station was designed by William Livlock in a restrained 'Barry-esque' Tuscan Doric style with a great arched roof 840 feet in length and spanning 212 feet, which was supported on single span trussed cast-iron arches each weighing 25 tons. When opened, it was described in *Aris's Gazette* as, 'the vast structure [that] merits the distinction of being the finest railway station in the world'.

Sadly, New Street's reputation as a fine station did not last too long. By the 1920s the LMS, formed after the Grouping of 1923, which brought the LNWR and Midland Railway together, received a number of complaints about the poor state of the station. The building suffered further after it was bombed during the Second World War and the roof over the LNWR section was removed. The station itself was extended in 1890, with another glass and iron arched roof over the new structure, to accommodate the trains of the Midland Railway. This roof survived intact until it was demolished in the 1960s to make way for the new New Street station.

(*Opposite*) By the early 1960s New Street had gained the reputation of being one of the worst stations in the country. At the same time, plans were in hand to electrify the West Coast Main Line, between London, Euston and Glasgow, and included the section from Rugby to Stafford via Birmingham. In 1964 all London traffic was rerouted via the GWR Snow Hill–Paddington line and New Street station was closed for rebuilding and electrification. Here, reconstruction is underway and the Burton's building in High Street, close to the road junction with New Street, can be seen in the background.

The interior of New Street station in LNWR days before the Midland Railway extension was added. While the station was being built the GWR showed an interest in sharing the new station with the LNWR and obtaining running powers over the Stour Valley Railway, then under construction, to Wolverhampton. This would have brought the broad gauge into New Street, something the LNWR was keen to prevent, and would also relieve the GWR of the necessity to construct its own route through the Black Country. Needless to say, the LNWR, who did everything they could to prevent the GWR reaching the West Midlands, would have nothing to do with the approach from Paddington, so two competing routes between Birmingham and Wolverhampton had to be built. Had the Birmingham powers that be insisted that there should only be one main station in Birmingham, then the LNWR would have had to negotiate with Paddington and much unpleasantness would have been avoided.

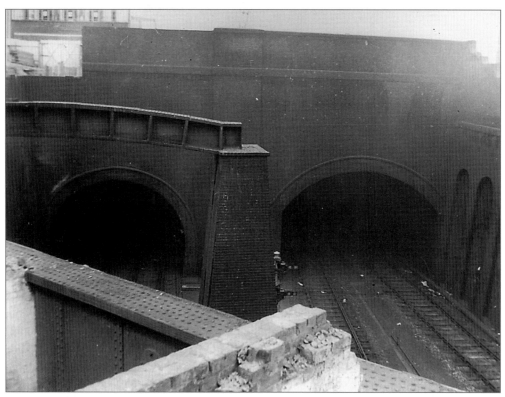

The south end tunnels approaching New Street station at the time when reconstruction work was underway.

A night-time view of the new New Street station, which opened in 1968. It was no more than a concrete slab with the shopping complex above, giving the station a low roof which fills with diesel fumes and is somewhat draughty. The new station is even less popular than the old one and there have been plans put forward to have this station replaced. It remains to be seen what the future holds for this unpopular structure.

The London end of the modern New Street station in the early 1980s with a Cross-City DMU train from Lichfield City, *en route* to Longbridge, arriving at the station. The Cross-City line between Lichfield and Longbridge, utilizing the old LNWR route between Lichfield and New Street and the Midland Railway's Birmingham West Suburban Railway (BWSR) and Birmingham and Gloucester Railway from King's Norton to a new station at Longbridge, was opened in 1978 and became the most used suburban railway outside London. In the background is the Birmingham landmark building known as the Rotunda that opened in the 1960s as part of the postwar rebuilding programme for the city centre. The Rotunda lies at the junction of Smallbrook Queensway, High Street and New Street, the thoroughfare from which the station obtained its name, rather than Navigation Street, which the LNWR had originally wanted to call it.

One of the suburban branches operated by the LNWR in Birmingham was the little line to Harborne. This reached its traffic peak in 1906 until competition from Birmingham Corporation trams and buses caused a major decline in traffic and the line became closed to passengers in 1934. The line remained open for freight until 1950, then it closed altogether. Here, Hagley Road station can be seen in the days before the First World War.

The terminus of the line was at Harborne, seen here with a local train, headed by a LNWR 0–6–2 tank loco, awaiting departure with a train for New Street.

On 3 June 1950 the Stephenson's Locomotive Society ran a railtour over the Harborne branch just after it closed, this being the first passenger train to operate over the little line since November 1934. The two-coach train is seen at Monument Lane as it is about to enter the branch. The locomotive used to haul this special was an ex-LNWR Webb 2–4–2 tank, no. 46757: these engines were a familiar sight on passenger trains that once operated over the line. The old branch is still in use – not as a railway route, but as a linear park which is popular with the local population.

Saltley locoshed on 2 March 1935 with 2P 4–4–0 no. 699, a London, Midland and Scottish Railway example of a locomotive type originally designed by the Midland Railway in 1912. Other locos of Midland design can also be seen in this view. A shed was established here in 1839, when the Birmingham and Derby Junction Railway, later to become part of the Midland empire, opened rudimentary accommodation in August of that year. A new locoshed, in the 'roundhouse' style, then much favoured by the Midland, was built in 1854 and given a facelift in 1864. Another shed was erected on a site a little further north in 1867 at a cost of £14,622, and further buildings were added in 1876 and 1900, making it the largest locoshed in Birmingham.

Saltley shed on 29 April 1956, with a line up of the locos that were used in the Birmingham area. In the foreground is 3F 0–6–0 no. 43523, a Midland-built loco of Henry Fowler design, and other 2F and 3F 0–6–0 tender engines. Just behind the 3F is a 2–6–0 'Crab' loco designed by George Hughes, ex-Chief Mechanical Engineer of the Lancashire and Yorkshire Railway. In Midland days the shed was coded 3 but became 21A after the Grouping, a coding it retained for the rest of its life. The shed was given a new roof under BR modernization in 1950; it closed on 6 March 1967.

Ex-Midland 1F 0–6–0 tank loco BR no. 41805 at Saltley shed, 1956. The shed provided locos for freight, local passenger and some express trains over the Midland lines in Birmingham as the allocation below shows.

Saltley Shed Allocations, November 1950

Diesel Shunters	12039, 12040, 12041, 12042, 12043, 12044, 12059, 12060, 12061, 12062, 12074, 12075, 12076, 12077
Stanier 2–6–2T	40097, 40115, 40117, 40171, 40175
MR 2P 4–4–0	40486, 40511
LMS 4P 'Compound' 4–4–0	40928
MR 4P 'Compound' 4–4–0	41035, 41046
MR 1F 0–6–0T	41699, 41856, 41879
Fairburn 2–6–4T	42053, 42054, 42141, 42685
Fowler 2–6–4T	42326, 42337
Hughes/Fowler 'Crab' 2–6–0	42754, 42758, 42764, 42790, 42818, 42822, 42824, 42825, 42826, 42827, 42829, 42857, 42890, 42900, 42903
'Ivatt' class 4 2–6–0	43011, 43014, 43043, 43044
MR 3F 0–6–0	43201, 43210, 43214, 43223, 43225, 43246, 43257, 43284, 43321, 43336, 43339, 43374, 43433, 43435, 43441, 43443, 43484, 43490, 43491, 43507, 43531, 43540, 43544, 43594, 43620, 43621, 43624, 43627, 43644, 43673, 43674, 43680, 43684, 43690, 43698, 43759, 43762, 43791, 43800, 43812
LMS 4F 0–6–0	43843, 43845, 43855, 43858, 43869, 43879, 43891, 43911, 43912, 43939, 43940, 43941, 43946, 43949, 43951, 43968, 43986, 44010, 44023, 44026, 44049, 44084, 44088, 44092, 44108, 44112, 44137, 44145, 44150, 44165, 44176, 44179, 44184, 44185, 44187, 44190, 44200, 44201, 44203, 44213, 44224, 44248, 44263, 44289, 44317, 44362, 44406, 44413, 44418, 44427, 44475, 44515, 44516, 44520, 44524, 44525, 44538, 44545, 44567, 44571, 44580, 44591
Black Five 4–6–0	44659, 44660, 44666, 44717, 44804, 44805, 44810, 44813, 44814, 44842, 44919, 44920, 44966, 45040, 45186, 45265, 45268, 45269, 45273, 45447
'Jinty' 0–6–0T	47276, 47301, 47313, 47638
LMS 8F 2–8–0	48319, 48336, 48339, 48351, 48388, 48401, 48417, 48420, 48424, 48669, 48687, 48700, 48763
MR Class 2 0–6–0	58167, 58230, 58231, 58261, 58271
	Total: 196

With Saltley locoshed and its coaling stage tower on the left, ex-LMS 4F 0–6–0 loco no. 44413 heads a southbound freight train past Landor Street Junction in 1956. The coaling stage seen here was provided under LMS modernization in 1936 together with a new ash plant.

A 1956 view of Landor Street Junction with an unidentified ex-LMS 'Jubilee' class 4–6–0 at the head of an express, probably a Bristol to Leeds train, the engine provided by the Bristol shed.

Moseley station, on the Camp Hill to King's Norton section of the Birmingham and Gloucester Railway, *c.* 1880. By this time passenger trains were terminating at the new Midland extension of New Street station. Initially, all trains terminated at Camp Hill until access to Curzon Street, the ex-L&B station, became available after New Street was opened. Later, space was found at New Street for the Midland trains terminus. The tunnel at Moseley was reputed to be the first covered way.

A turn-of-the-century view of Moseley station with a southbound Midland Railway train passing through. The opening of the Birmingham West Suburban Railway through to New Street in 1885 reduced the role of the B&G between New Street and King's Norton from an express route to a suburban line. As an economy measure, suburban passenger traffic was suspended on 27 January 1941. As there was no demand for reinstatement of such traffic on the New Street–King's Norton section, via Moseley, the line was abandoned as a suburban route in 1946. However, the line is still used for freight and as a useful bypass route for expresses between New Street and Bristol, avoiding modern Cross-City traffic. Moseley station suffered the indignity of bomb damage during the Blitz of 1940–1, which left it in a sorry state.

Bournville station on the Birmingham West Suburban Railway. A single line branch from Albion Wharf, near central Birmingham, to Lifford was authorized on 31 July 1871, with construction beginning shortly afterwards. The plans were then amended to terminate the line at Granville Street, thus avoiding the expense of having to bridge the Worcester and Birmingham canal to gain access to Albion Wharf. Bournville station, then named Stirchley Street, was opened with the new line on 1 April 1876.

While construction of the BWSR was underway, the line was taken over by the Midland Railway on 1 July 1875. The company extended the line into the new Midland extension at New Street station in 1885. At the same time the line was doubled and became the main express route for trains running between Derby and Bristol. The BWSR had stations at Church Road, Somerset Road, Selly Oak and Stirchley Street (Bournville), as well as the original terminus at Granville Street. Here, Bournville station is seen in Midland Railway days with a local train, headed by a 'Kirtley' 0–6–0, awaiting departure.

In the 1930s Cadbury's opened their factory to the public and visits to see the works proved very popular. In this view the first such excursion, run by the LMS at the time, is seen at Bournville station. The train is headed by an ex-MR 'Johnson' class 3 0–6–0. Note the proximity of the Birmingham and Worcester canal at this point, and the fashions of the day as visitors pose for the photograph.

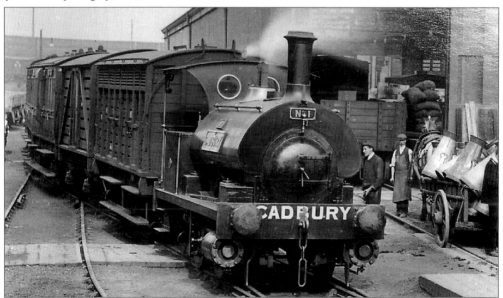

Cadbury's established their own railway in 1884 to link the works with the Worcester and Birmingham canal and the BWSR to allow easy transit of raw materials and finished products. Their early locomotives were 0–4–0 saddle tanks, one of which is seen here at the company's Waterside warehouse. It was not uncommon for large manufacturing companies to have their own railways to link with the main line system. The Austin works at nearby Longbridge also had its own railway for movement of finished cars, the company still using the main line railway to transport its completed products.

After the Second World War the railways began a decline that culminated in Dr Beeching recommending wholesale closures within the system in 1963. The BWSR survived as a main line express route, with trains transferred from the GWR Snow Hill–West Country route to the ex-Midland main line greatly increasing traffic. However, suburban services declined to only two each way a day by 1972. When the West Midland Passenger Transport Executive was formed, under the 1968 Transport Act, a proposal was put forward to develop the old LNWR line between New Street and Lichfield and the MR line from New Street to Redditch to form a Cross-City commuter line. Once approved, the two lines were developed and an intensive suburban service was operated from 1978. The service was very popular, becoming the most used railway outside London. Here, a four-car DMU set from Longbridge to Lichfield arrives at Bournville station.

Another Cross-City suburban train arrives at Bournville on its way to Longbridge. A new station was provided at Bournville, at a cost of £34,307, as part of Cross-City development. As the 1980s progressed there were complaints about overcrowding and the unreliability of these old DMU sets, many of which had been introduced in the 1950s, and plans were drawn up in 1990 to electrify the line at a cost of £18 million, with new Class 323 electric train sets on the route to operate suburban services. These eventually came into use in 1995 and the Cross-City line remains as popular as ever.

Closure of the old GWR main line between Birmingham and the West Country in 1962 brought extra express traffic to the ex-MR route via the Lickey Bank. Here, a West Country express, by a Class 47 Co-Co diesel-electric locomotive, thunders through Bournville station on its way to Bristol and beyond.

A Class 47-hauled express from the West Country slows as it enters Bournville station on its way to New Street in 1990. These express services have to avoid Cross-City suburban trains and at busy times are often re-routed over the old B&G route which avoids the BWSR altogether, connecting with the Bristol main line later at King's Norton.

In 1990 Cadbury's opened up a section of the factory as a museum called Cadbury World which attracts many thousands of visitors a year, some of whom come by rail. On the station at Bournville a sign has been erected to let passengers know that this is the location of the museum. Indeed, Bournville station is painted in the purple of the Cadbury company, with 'glass and a half' symbols attached to the fence.

The entrance to Bournville station is from the road below. Here we can see the entrance from Bournville Lane after it was redeveloped as part of Cross-City improvements. The railway crosses the road, along with the Worcester and Birmingham Canal, on a low, narrow bridge, as can be seen here. This bridge only allows single-decker buses to pass underneath and for many years the no. 27 route, between West Heath and King's Heath, was the only single-deck bus service in the city.

As part of Cross-City development a brand new station was opened on the main New Street–Bristol line at Longbridge, seen here on a Sunday afternoon in November 1994 with an Inter-City 125 train set rushing through the station on its way to the West Country. A station had existed at Longbridge on the Halesowen branch, which closed to passengers in 1919, but had been retained for use by works trains until 1958, when such services were withdrawn. The line, however, was retained for freight use until 1964 when it was closed altogether. The Austin works retained a stub to connect the factory with the main line so that finished motor cars could be transported to many parts of the country, thereby cutting down on road traffic. Part of the old Halesowen branch has been taken over by the company and the factory that built the Metro car is on the site. There was a suggestion that the old Halesowen branch should be opened again as far as Frankley, so that a connection could be made between a new housing estate there and the Cross-City line, but nothing came of the idea.

A Birmingham-bound Inter-City 125 enters Longbridge new station on the fast line in November 1994. Electrification of the Cross-City line was completed by this time and the poles supporting the 25kv overhead wires can be seen in this view.

Having been thwarted by the LNWR in its attempts to share New Street station the Great Western Railway had to find its own route into Birmingham by taking control of the Birmingham and Oxford Junction Railway. Its broad gauge line arrived in a temporary station at Snow Hill in 1852. This proved to be inadequate and a new one was built in 1871, the wooden structure moving to Didcot. The construction of a brand new station, the best known in the city, was commenced in 1906 and is the one seen in this view, with the Great Western Hotel, designed by J.A. Chatwin, in the foreground. Livery Street junction with Colmore Row can also be seen, with an electric tram on the left about to enter Colmore Row. The hotel became offices when the new station was opened with a restaurant alongside on the ground floor.

Snow Hill station viewed from Snow Hill itself, with a busy Colmore Row on the left. The GWR went on to open a terminus station at nearby Moor Street to cope with suburban traffic generated by the opening of the North Warwickshire Railway in 1908. Until Moor Street was opened in 1909, all traffic was dealt with at Snow Hill but the narrowness of this site precluded extension. Snow Hill station closed in 1972, much to the anguish of the Birmingham population, who argued that the station should be retained because they felt that New Street could not cope with the demands placed upon it. They appear to have been proved right: a new Snow Hill was opened in the late 1980s, albeit as a suburban halt. Moor Street was retained until 1987, when a new station was opened as part of developments at Snow Hill, on the main line to Bordesley.

Small Heath and Sparkbrook station, on the line between Snow Hill, Moor Street and Tyseley, 1950s. When the GWR approached Birmingham the LNWR insisted that a connection should be made between the B&OJ and their main line into New Street and that the B&OJ line should be mixed gauge as far as Leamington to allow the LNWR access over the new route. This was sheer bloody-mindedness to make the GWR access to Birmingham as difficult as possible. The mixed gauge line was laid and a viaduct was constructed towards New Street, at a point between Bordesley and Snow Hill, but was never completed, the LNWR insisting that work should stop once it entered their property. This viaduct is still standing and has never had a length of rail laid on it. It can be seen on the left after leaving Moor Street station, and is testament to the spite of the LNWR who could not have their own way.

Ex-GWR Churchward 2–6–0 no. 5386 awaits access into Small Heath goods yard in July 1956 with a freight train. The houses in the background have now disappeared to make way for a new road.

Tyseley station was opened in 1908 to cope with traffic generated from the new North Warwickshire Railway. In the distance, the junction of the B&OJ to Paddington can be seen curving away to the left and the North Warwickshire line curving away to the right. The signal-box controlling the junction can be seen through the overbridge.

Tyseley station, looking towards Snow Hill. On the right is a large goods shed from where locally built motorcycles, from such manufacturers as Velocette and James, were despatched all over the UK. Tyseley locoshed, opened in 1908, can be seen on the left. The shed was also a factory that undertook heavy repairs until such work was transferred to the Wolverhampton Stafford Road works in the 1930s. Repair work to the shed's allocation was still done there until it closed in 1969.

The first station on the North Warwickshire Railway is at Spring Road, Tyseley, seen here in the 1970s looking towards Tyseley itself. The Birmingham and North Warwickshire Railway, to give it its proper title, was originally promoted to run from Stratford-upon-Avon to a new station at Birmingham (Moor Street) but promoters could not raise the necessary capital to fund the project. It was eventually taken over by the GWR who built the line from Tyseley to Bearley North Junction, where it met the B&OJ branch from Hatton to Stratford via Wilmcote. When opened in 1908 it was a double track line and became an express route to Bristol and Cardiff, avoiding the rather circuitous route via Solihull, Hatton and Bearley. It was also a useful suburban line as Birmingham businessmen moved out of the city and into the countryside. The line was scheduled for closure under Beeching but survives as a commuter line and is now part of a new Cross-City route via Snow Hill to Stourbridge.

Following the closure of Tyseley shed in 1969 all buildings, except one turntable and the coaling stage, were demolished. These facilities were then taken over by the Birmingham Standard Gauge Steam Trust who had recently bought ex-Western Region 'Castle' class loco no. 7029 *Clun Castle* and wanted the facilities to house her. From that time, with assistance from Birmingham City Council, the Tyseley centre has become established as an important railway museum and workshop and has been used for Youth Training and Employment Training schemes. I recall a young lady boilersmith working on the boiler of another Castle, no. 5080 *Defiant*, as she underwent restoration to full working order. Here, in 1985, *Clun Castle* is on the turntable after working an excursion over the North Warwickshire line from Stratford-upon-Avon.

A view of the museum at Tyseley with the Trust's own ex-GWR saddle tank along with 'Tiny', the smallest standard gauge loco, and ex-Metropolitan Railway no. 1 0–8–2 tank loco, in 1986.

A view of the main Moor Street–Paddington line at Tyseley in 1987 with a Class 58 diesel-electric loco at the head of a coal train heading south. Also in view is a DMU set, used on local services between Moor Street and Stratford/Leamington Spa.

Ex-GWR 'Collett Hall' class 4–6–0 no. 4983 *Albert Hall* awaits restoration at Tyseley museum in 1987. This loco was modelled by Hornby for many years so it will be good to see the original in full working order.

Ex-LMS 'Jubilee' class 4–6–0 *Kolhapur* at Stratford-upon-Avon in 1986. This loco was restored by the Tyseley workshops in 1985 with funding from Birmingham City Council.

Ex-LMS Stanier 'Princess-Coronation' Pacific no. 46235 *City of Birmingham* at the Museum of Science and Industry. The locomotive was given to the city by BR in the 1960s. The museum also has a nameplate from ex-GWR 'Atbarn' class 4–4–0 *City of Birmingham*, sister engine to *City of Truro*, the first engine to reach 100 mph in 1904.

CHAPTER THREE

BIRMINGHAM CITY TRANSPORT

Between 1904 and 1969 navy blue and primrose liveried vehicles of Birmingham City Transport were a common sight on the city's streets, all carrying the Birmingham coat of arms with its 'Forward' motto. Until the early 1950s the bulk of the city's fleet were electric trams, first introduced on the Bristol Road route in 1900 under the auspices of the City of Birmingham Tramway Company. From that time the electric tramway system expanded as far as Dudley and Wednesbury, in the Black Country, while within Birmingham the system operated to Erdington and Short Heath in the north of the city and as far as Rubery, Rednal and Cotteridge in the south. There were also routes to Hall Green, Stechford, Acocks Green, Alum Rock and Washwood Heath, to name but a few destinations. Unusually, the tramway system operated on the 3 ft 6 in gauge rather than the standard of 4 ft 8½ in, which was the norm elsewhere in Britain.

Prior to the introduction of electric trams, horse-drawn trams operated from Colmore Row to Hockley Brook as an extension of the 4 ft 8½ in gauge Dudley Port to Hockley Brook service from 11 September 1873. The horse tramway never really took off in Birmingham and steam trams became widespread from 1882 to 1886. From 1888 a cable-operated tramway opened between Colmore Row and New Inns, Handsworth, and a lead-acid battery-operated tramway ran along the Bristol Road from 1890. All were converted to electric traction from 1900, the battery system needing to be replaced because passengers complained of fumes. Despite the popularity of Birmingham's trams, the last ran within the city in 1953.

One tram route, that along the Coventry Road which was considered to be a financial burden, was converted to trolleybus operation, from 1934 until 30 June 1951.

Not all of Birmingham's public transport services were operated by trams. Many people in better off areas considered them to be the transport of the working class and buses operated over the streets of the expanding city in the early years of Birmingham City Transport. Early vehicles tended to be AEC buses with Short Brothers bodies and open staircases. AEC vehicles continued to be used right up to the 1930s, many being maintained at the ex-Midland Red depot in Tennant Street, near Five Ways. By the mid-1930s Daimler COG5 double-deck and single-deck buses were added to the fleet, some lasting until the early 1960s. After the Second World War the bus fleet was rapidly expanded as the city decided to abandon its trams. From 1946 Daimler CV6 buses began to appear in ever-increasing numbers in Birmingham, along with Leyland PD2 and Crossley buses. From 1952 identical Metropolitan-Cammell-bodied Daimler, Crossley and Guy buses became a common sight on the city streets. Rear-engined Daimler Fleetline and Leyland Atlantean buses began trials in Birmingham during the early 1960s, along with an unusual AEC vehicle (the only one built), the latter not finding favour. Indeed, during the postwar period of bus expansion, only a few AEC Regent vehicles were purchased by the city, these operating over the Stratford Road routes. The engines on these vehicles had a strange 'whistle'.

Birmingham City Transport disappeared as an entity in 1969 following the 1968 Transport Act. This created seven transport executives in England who were responsible for operating both local bus and train services. Under the act, the bus services of Birmingham, West Bromwich, Wolverhampton and Coventry came under the auspices of the West Midlands Passenger Transport Executive and Birmingham's bus livery changed to primrose and mid-blue with a 'WM' logo replacing the coat of arms. Bus deregulation in the 1980s brought about the creation of West Midland Travel and a new livery of silver grey, mid-blue and red. However, as a reminder of bygone days, some new buses have now been painted in the old Birmingham City Transport colours, complete with the 'Forward' coat of arms.

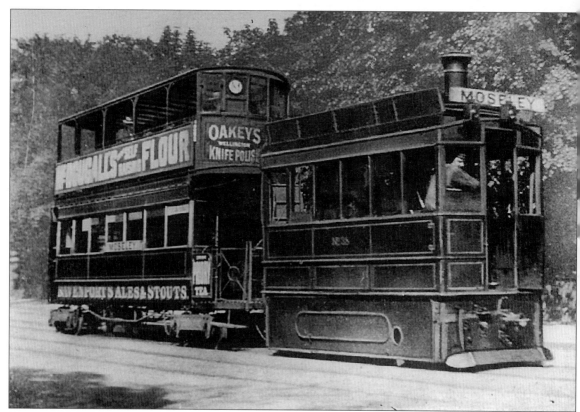

A steam tram locomotive and double-deck trailer on the route to Moseley, which opened on 29 December 1884. Steam tram operation in Birmingham dated back to January 1876 when a tram locomotive, designed by John Downes of Birmingham and built by Henry Hughes, Falcon Works, Loughborough, Leicestershire, in 1875, was used experimentally on the Birmingham Snow Hill–West Bromwich and Hill Top (Wednesbury) services. The first regular steam tram operation was between Old Square, near Lewis's, and Witton, which started on Boxing Day 1882 and was run by the Birmingham and Aston Tramway Company. The Birmingham Central Tramway Company, later the City of Birmingham Tramway Company, began operating steam trams to Perry Barr from 25 November 1884, followed by its route to Moseley. Further double-deck steam tram routes were opened: along the Stratford Road from 11 May 1885, and the Coventry Road from 16 January 1886. The Birmingham and Midland Tramways Company opened a route on 6 July 1885 from Lionel Street, close to Birmingham city centre, and along the Dudley Road to the city boundary; this route was soon extended to Oldbury, West Bromwich, and Dudley. All of these routes were on 3 ft 6 in gauge track, which was to become the standard for all future Birmingham tramways. Steam traction continued to develop, an extension along the Stratford Road opened as late as 1899, and coke refuelling points were situated at each terminus. However, development of electric traction elsewhere meant that the days of the steam tram were numbered. Between 1904 and 1907 the steam tram routes were converted to electric operation as the municipally owned Birmingham City Tramways took control of all tram operations.

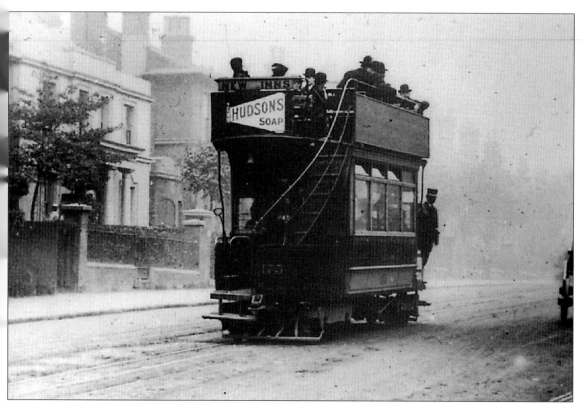

Another Edwardian view of the New Inns cable tram. Here, tram no. 175 speeds towards Handsworth on a dull day. On wet days these open-top vehicles must have been rather uncomfortable for upstairs passengers.

Cable trams at New Inns, Handsworth, with Handsworth library in the background. This line, from Colmore Row to New Inns via Hockley, was opened on 24 March 1888, replacing a standard gauge tramway. Trams no. 94 and no. 95 are seen in this Edwardian view (judging by the fashions displayed).

An open-topped electric tram on the Coventry Road route at Small Heath. This was not far from the St Andrews Ground of Birmingham City FC (then known as Birmingham FC), which was opened on Boxing Day 1906.

Open-topped electric trams, nos 183 and 186, at Yardley, on the Coventry Road. The Coventry Road tramway terminus in the city centre was at Station Street. From 29 March 1904 the electric tramcars, run by the City of Birmingham Tramways Company, originally operated from Small Heath. From here they connected with steam trams from the city, through Hay Mills, where the city boundary was then situated, to Church Road, South Yardley. A steam tram service from the city to Small Heath Park had been running since January 1888. From 23 February 1905 (around the time that this picture was taken) a full electric service was operated from Station Street to South Yardley. Trams operating over the route were ex-Radial Class 71s or smaller Brills of the 21 or 221 Class. By 1932 the Coventry Road route was considered to be something of a financial burden, so in 1933 the Birmingham Corporation decided to convert the route to trolleybus operation and ordered fifty Leyland TTBD2 six-wheeled trolleybuses. These were bodied locally by Metropolitan-Cammell of Washwood Heath, the largest trolleybus order ever. The no. 15 tram service then became trolleybus service no. 92. The trolleybus route itself was abandoned on 30 June 1951. In view in this picture is the Swan Hotel; in the 1890s this building, in its mock-Elizabethan style, had replaced an old coaching inn of 1605. This newer building was itself replaced in 1967 by an ugly concrete structure whose only claim to fame was that it had the longest bar counter in the world. Even this modern building has now disappeared.

Open-topped trams, nos 22 and 214, on the Birmingham–Windmill Lane route. These open-topped cars were built in 1905 and were probably new in this view. They had four-bay bodies mounted on Brill 22E bogies and had Dick Kerr 25hp motors. Top covers were fitted between 1905 and 1907 but they remained with open balconies. The platforms were vestibuled and normal stairs, instead of the reverse kind, were fitted in 1924 and 1929. These trams remained in service until they were withdrawn in December 1949. In this busy scene the only other traction in view is horse power.

(*Opposite*) Two views of an open-topped tramcar decorated for King Edward VII's visit to Birmingham on 7 July 1909. When I first saw these photographs I wondered what the 'A.R.' stood for but it occurred to me that the king's name was actually 'Albert Edward'. Having said that, the king's wife was named Alexandra so the initials could refer to her. Illuminated trams were not a common feature in the city and the last such tram to run over the city's routes was in 1945, to celebrate Britain's victory in the Second World War.

An open-topped electric tramcar operating over the leafy Bristol Road route. Originally a horse tramway, this route was converted to electric traction in 24 July 1890. Unusually, the method of traction used was electric accumulator cars, twelve such vehicles being built for the service from the city to Dawlish Road, Selly Oak. These vehicles were not a great success because their batteries frequently failed. However, they continued to operate until 14 May 1901. In 1900 the City of Birmingham Tramways Company offered to replace the battery powered cars with overhead electric trams. This meant that trials with overhead systems had to be carried out for eleven years because of leasing agreements between the company and Birmingham Corporation. The new overhead system began operations from 14 May 1901, using fifteen cars built by the Electric Railway & Tramway Carriage Works Ltd. These new trams operated from Suffolk Street, in the centre of the city, to Chapel Lane, Selly Oak, half a mile further on than the old accumulator cars. From that time all of the city's trams were converted to the overhead system.

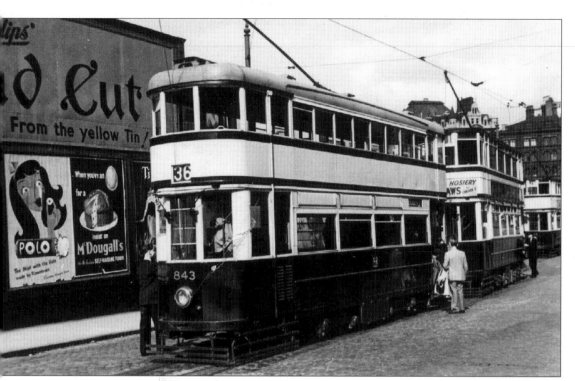

At the Navigation Street terminus of the no. 36 route to Cotteridge, via Pebble Mill Road and the Pershore Road, is car No. 843, a Brush-built, totally enclosed lightweight tramcar, which went into service in 1930 and was withdrawn in January 1952. It had a seating capacity of sixty (thirty-three on the upper deck and twenty-seven on the lower deck) and was mounted on M.&T. Burnley bogies with GEC WT28AS 40hp motors.

Tramcar no. 828 at Navigation Street on the Cotteridge service. A Short Brothers vehicle of 1929, this car survived until July 1952, when the tram service to Cotteridge was replaced by the no. 45 bus service.

Another view of car no. 843 at Navigation Street on the no. 36 service to Cotteridge. Judging by this picture, the livery suggests that the car is new into service. The pre-war primrose underpanel is present, while the previous tramcar pictured has the underpanel in postwar navy.

ebble Mill Road junction, the point where Bristol Road and Pershore Road services divided, is now the site of the BBC Birmingham headquarters. A row of trams, headed by car no. 793, a 1928 Brush-built vehicle, waits in the reserved area nd a Rover car, built in nearby Solihull, is parked on the grass verge. This particular tram was withdrawn in 1952.

Trams nos 818 and 823 on the no. 36 service at Pebble Mill Road in June 1952, the final year of tram operations. Cannon Hill Park and Edgbaston cricket ground, the home of Warwickshire CCC, are close by.

Pebble Mill Road junction with Cotteridge-bound tram no. 36 in the foreground and two trams in the distance. Also i view is a Longbridge-built Austin saloon car. This picture was taken in June 1952, the last year of tram operations ove this route.

Tramcar no. 812, a Brush vehicle with a Short Bros body, on the no. 36 service heading towards the city centre from Cotteridge and passing through Stirchley. Another tram bound for Cotteridge can be seen in the distance.

Another Brush-built and Short-bodied tram, no. 824, has arrived at the Cotteridge terminus and is ready to depart for Navigation Street. A tram depot was situated in Cotteridge which later became a depot for buses, supplying vehicles for the nos 41, 45 and 47 bus routes. Sadly this bus garage has now closed.

Back at Navigation Street and tramcar no. 737, a 1926 Brush-built vehicle, is on the no. 70 service to Rednal on Christmas Day 1951. This service ran along the Bristol Road to the favourite 'Brummie' playground at the Lickey Hills and, in the summer months, was very busy taking the Birmingham populace to their favourite rural spot.

Leaving Navigation Street and entering John Bright Street, tram no. 529, 1913/14-built and originally with open balconies, enclosed in about 1930, is on the no. 35 service to Selly Oak on 7 June 1952. Just to the right of the tram is Finlay's tobacco kiosk, a landmark on Navigation Street for many years, and on the left is a Daimler CVG6 bus, brought into service to replace the trams. The entrance to New Street station is also close to this point.

On 15 September 1937 open-balconied tramcar no. 341 on the no. 35 Selly Oak service awaits departure back to Navigation Street after arriving at the Selly Oak terminus. This particular vehicle was built in 1911 and withdrawn in 1950.

On 7 June 1952 tramcar no. 767, on the service to Pebble Mill Road, leaves Selly Oak garage at the Chapel Lane/Bristol Road junction. Also in view is another tram on the no. 35 service from Selly Oak to Navigation Street, and two Daimler CV6 buses.

Tramcar no. 795 heads down Bristol Road, Selly Oak, on the no. 72 service from the Austin works at Longbridge (a short working of the no. 70 service to Rednal) to Navigation Street. The tram is about to pass under the railway bridge that carries the Birmingham West Suburban Railway from New Street to King's Norton as it enters Selly Oak station.

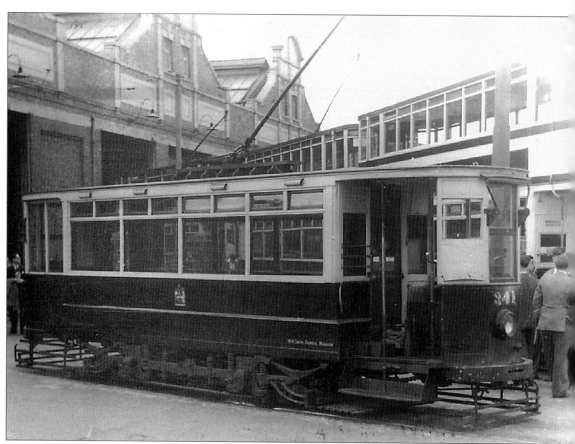

Selly Oak tram depot as it appeared on 17 June 1951, with single-deck departmental car no. 341 in the foreground. Selly Oak depot was opened on 12 July 1927 and its ten roads had the capacity for eighty trams. Situated in Chapel Lane and Harborne Lane it replaced a forty-tram capacity depot at Bournbrook. The new depot was required because tram routes had been extended in recent years and a larger fleet of vehicles was required. The Bristol Road routes had been extended from Selly Oak to Northfield on 1 October 1923, to Longbridge on 17 December 1923, to Rednal (and the Lickey Hills) on 14 April 1924, and to Rubery on 8 February 1926. The Dutch-style gabled building remained as a tram depot until 5 July 1952, although it had been a bus garage as well from 2 January 1935. It remained as a bus garage when the trams were withdrawn from service providing buses for the no. 62 (Rednal) and no. 63 (Rubery) services, which replaced tram services nos 35, 69 (Northfield), 70, 71 (Rubery) and 72. The depot also supplied single-deck buses for the no. 27 service, which ran from West Heath to King's Heath via Bournville. Single-deck vehicles had to be used over this route because of the low bridge that carried the BWSR into Bournville station and the Worcester and Birmingham Canal over Bournville Lane. From the mid-1930s single-deck Daimler COG5 buses ran the service, until 1950 when they were replaced by Leyland Tiger PS2 buses and full-fronted Leyland Olympics. From the mid-1960s rear-engined Daimler Fleetline buses replaced the old Leyland vehicles. The depot at Selly Oak was finally closed in the 1980s and remains derelict. It was at this depot, in the early 1960s, that I discovered a Daimler COG5 double-decker bus, dating from about 1935. Its seats had been removed and it was presumably to be converted into a breakdown vehicle, a common fate for these long-lived buses.

On 25 May 1952 trams no. 748 and no. 833 pass under the BWSR railway bridge, Bristol Road, Selly Oak, one heading towards Navigation Street and the other, on service no. 70, going to Rednal. In the background is the building and clock tower of the University of Birmingham which was opened on 7 July 1909, the brainchild of the famous Birmingham MP Joseph Chamberlain. The new university replaced the original Josiah Mason-inspired college in Edmund Street. The Arts faculty of the university remained at Edmund Street until the building was demolished in 1963, at which time the whole of the university was united on the Edgbaston campus.

Tramcar no. 798 heads away from Rednal and towards Longbridge on the leafy central reservation of the Bristol Road, as it travels back to the city centre, 1952.

Tramcar no. 381, a UEC-built open balcony vehicle, in service from 1912 until 1950, is at the Rednal terminus – and gateway to the Lickey Hills – of the no. 70 service. The terminus was well known for its grand wrought-iron and glass waiting shelters. It also had a large loop to accommodate the huge number of trams that were often required in the summer months as thousands of Brummies descended on the Lickey Hills on weekend afternoons. As the hundreds queued to return home after their day out, Selly Oak depot could not supply all the vehicles needed and trams from Cotteridge depot, along with some from Moseley Road, would be pressed into service. Birmingham City Transport had a notice at the end of the glass shelters, advising passengers to return early to guarantee catching a tram and warning them that the last tram left at 10 p.m.

Tram no. 828 waits at the Rednal terminus on 6 January 1938, the service relatively quiet during the winter months. Along with the waiting shelters, now sadly disappeared, the terminus also provided toilet facilities. The building is now a café and visitor's centre.

A view of the impressive terminus at Rednal, with a tram waiting to return to Navigation Street at the end of the shelter. This terminus was set in an attractive location with a lawn and flowerbeds surrounded by trees. The Lickey Hills themselves can be seen in the background. They were bequeathed to the city by the Cadbury family for recreational purposes only and they remain popular with the people of Birmingham today.

Travelling along the Hagley Road is open balcony tramcar no. 382, built in 1911. This service ran from Fountain Road along the Hagley Road to Navigation Street. The service began operating as a First Class service from 15 February 1914 to 19 May 1914, continuing as the no. 34 service until 9 August 1930 when it was replaced by the no. 95 buses. During the interwar years open balcony trams were popular with children, particularly on the Rednal service to the Lickey Hills in the summer.

A busy scene at Soho Road, Handsworth, with Birmingham Corporation trams for Colmore Row picking up passengers. In the background is the Council House and library. Before its absorption into the city of Birmingham in 1911, Handsworth was in the borough of Aston Manor and an agreement was reached between Birmingham and the borough for through-tram operations, the city actually operating tram services from 1907. Tram services nos 26 (Colmore Row to Oxhill Road), 27 (Colmore Row to Stafford Road, Handsworth) and 28 (Colmore Row to New Inns) all operated along the Soho Road. All of these tram services were replaced by the no. 71 bus service from 1 April 1939.

Colmore Row, in the heart of the Birmingham business district, with tram no. 551, built in 1913/14, on the no. 24 service from Colmore Row to Lozells via Wheeler Street and Hampstead Road. This service was abandoned on 7 August 1933. Just visible in the left background is the Great Western Railway station, Snow Hill. Nowadays Colmore Row is the terminus for all night service buses.

On the no. 79 Steelhouse Lane to Pype Hayes Park service, tram no. 728, a 1925 Brush-built vehicle, is seen close to its destination. The line opened on 20 July 1927 and was abandoned on 4 July 1953, being replaced by the no. 66 bus route.

A pair of tramcars, headed by no. 642, a 1923 MRCW-built vehicle on the no. 78 Steelhouse Lane–Short Heath service, await departure. The rear vehicle is on the no. 79 service.

Two trams await departure from the Steelhouse Lane terminus of the no. 79 service. This service commenced on 27 July 1927 and was abandoned in 1953. In the background is the Gaumont Cinema.

An unidentified open balcony tramcar on the no. 84 Albert street to Stechford (Stuarts Road) service, via Deritend and Coventry Road. This service began on 26 August 1928 and was abandoned on 2 October 1948, being replaced by the no. 54 bus service.

Tramcar no. 843, built in 1930, is seen on special duties ahead of tramcar no. 358, a 1911-built open balcony vehicle, on the no. 84 Stechford service.

Several 1911-built open-balcony tramcars. Nos 358 and 373 can be seen here, the first being on the no. 84 service. These UEC top-covered four-bay bodied cars had a seating capacity of fifty-two, twenty-eight on the top deck and twenty-four on the lower deck. The bodies were mounted on UEC 7 feet 6 inch swing-yoke trucks with Dick Kerr DK 13A 40hp motors. These vehicles were all withdrawn by October 1950. One of this class, no. 395, has been preserved at the Birmingham Museum of Science and Industry, the only Birmingham tram to be saved to date.

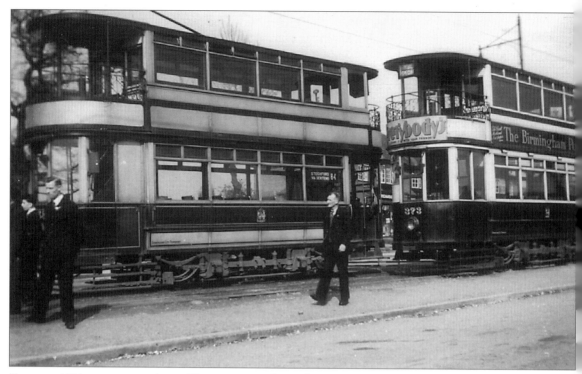

Two more 1911 trams, one on the no. 84 route, are seen here. The rear tram is no. 373.

Another view of tramcar no. 373, this time ready to be used on a special football service, probably taking Birmingham City supporters from St Andrews to the city centre.

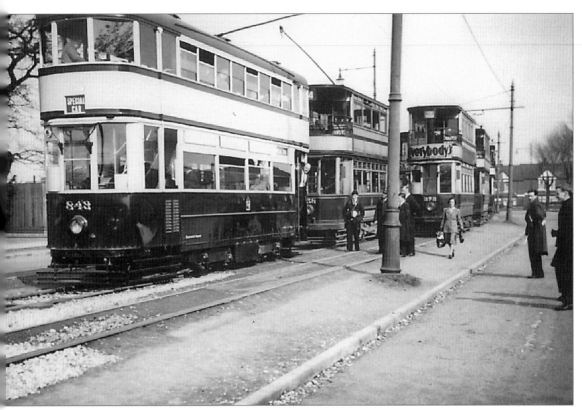

A row of the city's trams, headed by car no. 843. Also in view is car no. 373.

Car no. 70, built in 1905, on the no. 90 Stechford service. Cars of this class were withdrawn between July 1930 and March 1937.

The no. 90 tram service on reserve track at the Stuarts Lane terminus in Stechford.

Tramcar no. 728, a Brush-built vehicle of 1926, on the no. 2 service from Steelhouse Lane to Erdington (Chester Road). The service began on 24 April 1907. From 25 September 1938 this service was diverted from High Street, Erdington, to Sutton New Road. The line was abandoned on 4 July 1953 and replaced by the no. 64 bus service.

Running into Ladywood, tramcar no. 748, another 1926-built Brush vehicle, operates the no. 33 Navigation Street–Ladywood (Icknield Port Road) service. This was abandoned on 30 August 1947 and replaced by the no. 95 Ladywood bus service. The bus service was operated by Leyland PO2 vehicles.

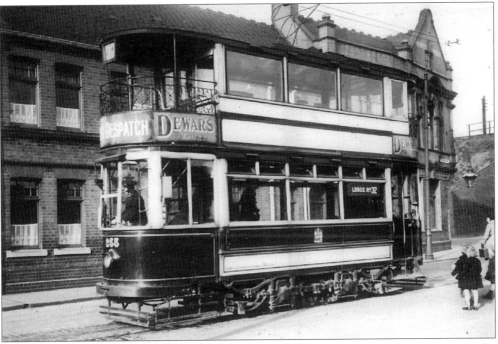

The no. 32 Lodge Road tram service, here being operated by tramcar no. 255. This route was one of the most tortuous in the city and, as a result of a fatal accident in Warstone Lane on 1 October 1907, only the smallest four-wheeled vehicles were used. The tram service itself was abandoned on 29 March 1947 and replaced by the no. 96 bus service. This bus route was used for trials of a Leyland 'Atlantean' rear-engined vehicle in the early 1960s.

The no. 6 Perry Barr service, operated, appropriately by tramcar no. 6, a 1903-built vehicle, which was withdrawn in 1949. The line was abandoned on 21 December 1949 and the route was incorporated into the existing no. 33 bus service.

Tramcar no. 158, an open balcony car built in 1906, on the no. 13 service (High Street to Small Heath Park). This was one of the routes that was replaced by trolleybuses from 6 January 1934.

Operating the no. 42 service, High Street to Alcester Lanes End via Bradford Street, is tramcar no. 442, built in 1904 and withdrawn in 1939. The line was abandoned in 1949 and replaced by the no. 50 bus service.

The no. 37 Cannon Hill tram service, which operated from Navigation Street to Willows Road, was abandoned on 1 October 1949 and replaced by the no. 48 bus service. Here, the tram service is being operated by car no. 726.

Another no. 37 service to Cannon Hill, serving the park and Warwickshire county cricket ground at Edgbaston, operated by car no. 725.

Open balcony car no. 419, with front passengers watching the photographer, on the no. 37 service. This picture must have been taken during the Second World War as the headlight has a cover to prevent light being shown at night.

Leaving Witton depot with an enthusiasts' special is car no. 623 on 28 June 1953. These enthusiasts' specials, taking fans of trams over local routes, were run in Birmingham just before the trams were laid off.

The Birmingham Corporation's coat of arms as it appeared on all of their tramcars.

Permanent Way car no. 8, early 1930s. Behind is an AEC Regent double-decker bus.

A vehicle repairing the overhead wires, 18 May 1939.

Tramcar no. 757, a Brush-built vehicle of 1926 and withdrawn from service in 1952, appears to be at the top of Streetley Road, Short Heath.

A good view of tramcar no. 616, a Brush-built vehicle of 1920/1. Originally built with open balconies, these vehicles were enclosed in the late 1920s. This tram and the whole class were withdrawn between 1949 and 1953.

The junction of Smallbrook Street (on the right) and Holloway Head on 25 May 1952. A tram from Navigation Street approaches in the distance, while car no. 754 on the no. 71 service from Rubery unloads passengers before it goes on to the Navigation Street terminus.

A pre-First World War view of Five Ways. This was the Birmingham boundary in 1807 and in 1840 tolls were still taken for the upkeep of the highway. Trams from Ladywood crossed here, as does the no. 95 bus service today.

Car no. 623 runs up what appears to be Bradford Street with a special service on 28 June 1953. To the left is a Longbridge-built Austin A40 Somerset, registration number KOE 295.

Slade Road, Stockland Green, the tram service here beginning on Sunday 12 June 1907; this view appears to have been taken shortly after its opening. Indeed, so quiet is the road that two mothers appear to be happy pushing their prams along it rather than using the pavement. This is something that would not be possible today, given that the road would be full of cars, lorries and buses.

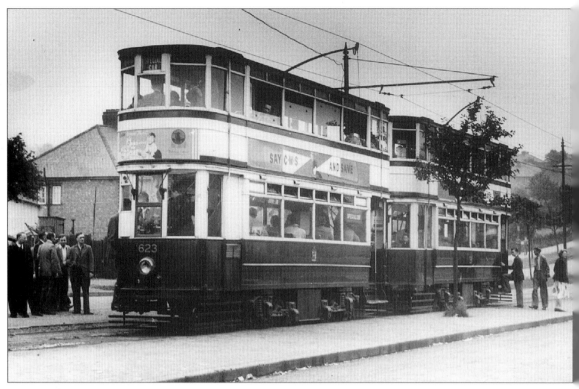

Two tramcars on enthusiasts' specials, headed by no. 623, are on reserved track at Short Heath in June 1953.

Car no. 616 on special duties turns from Bull Street into High Street, past the Beehive shop (like a department store, only cheaper), made famous by comedian Jasper Carrott, who told many stories of his time working there. In the background is a 1952-built Daimler CVG6 bus, one of those brought in to replace the trams.

Tramcar no. 625 out of Birmingham at Dudley, in the heart of the Black Country, on the no. 74 service from Livery Street. The line ran from Birmingham via West Bromwich and was abandoned on 1 April 1939, being replaced by a bus service with the same number.

Two rows of tramcars, headed by car no. 521, are on the no. 23 service from Colmore Row to the Hawthorns, home of West Bromwich Albion Football Club. Presumably these trams are lined up to bring football fans back to the city after a match.

Tramcar no. 89, a 1906-built open balcony car, travels along the Hagley Road on the no. 29 service to Bearwood. Although most of the class was withdrawn in 1939 this vehicle, along with a few others, was retained for emergency duties during the Second World War.

Another tramcar, no. 191, on the no. 29 service from Edmund Street to Bearwood. This service began on 1 April 1928 and was run jointly with the Midland Red. It ceased operating on 30 September 1939, being replaced by the B82 bus service. This particular tramcar was one of those scrapped in 1939.

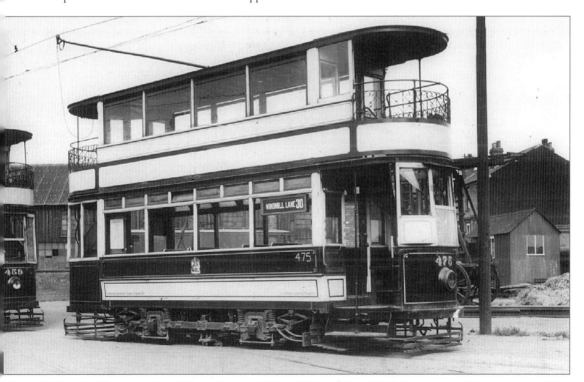

The no. 30 Smethwick service, from Edmund Street to Windmill Lane, Cape Hill, is here operated by tramcar no. 475, a 1903-built vehicle that was withdrawn in 1938. This service began on 1 July 1906; it was abandoned on 30 September 1939 and replaced by the B81 bus service. This was another route operated jointly with the Midland Red, although Birmingham Corporation actually ran all the vehicles.

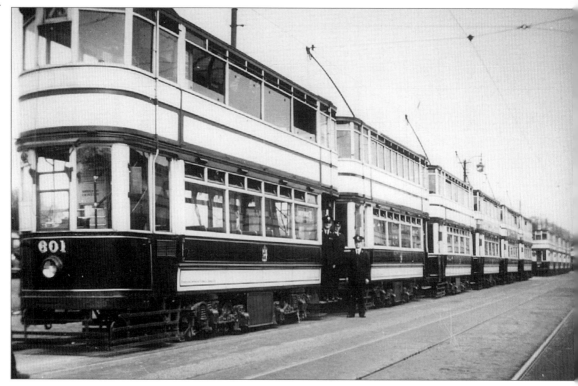

A row of trams at Carters Green, West Bromwich, headed by car no. 601, on the no. 73 service. This service was abandoned with all of the Black Country services in 1939 and replaced by the no. 73 bus service.

Tramcar no. 551, built in 1913 and withdrawn in about 1952, is seen operating the no. 74 service to Dudley.

Car no. 632 on reserved track at Short Heath on 30 December 1952. The track ran through a central area in the middle of the road that was reserved for trams. Therefore, no cars or lorries could be parked on it.

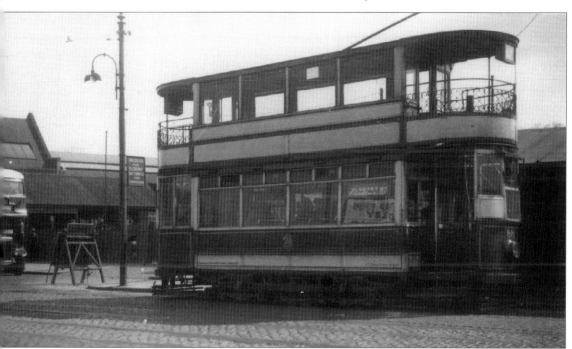

Tramcar no. 88 at the Dudley terminus of the no. 87 service. This route ran from Edmund Street to Dudley (Tipton Road) via Smethwick and Oldbury. It was taken over from the Midland Red by Birmingham City Transport on 1 April 1938 and it lasted as a tram service until 30 September 1939 when it was replaced by the B87 bus service. Behind the tram is a West Bromwich Corporation bus, probably a Guy vehicle, built in Wolverhampton. Many of the services running between Birmingham and the Black Country were jointly operated by Birmingham Corporation and West Bromwich Corporation, bringing the blue and white liveried West Bromwich vehicles into the city. In the post-Second World War years, Leyland PD2 double-decker buses operated most of the Black Country services for Birmingham Corporation.

On 18 April 1948 1930-built Brush lightweight car no. 843 is seen on special duties. This vehicle was withdrawn in January 1952 after a life of only twenty-two years. Heading in the opposite direction is a Daimler COG5 double decker bus.

The last day of tram operations in Birmingham, Saturday 4 July 1953. Car no. 608 is on service no. 79 at Lichfield Road, where passengers were transferred to waiting buses, the tram then going to Witton depot and its fate.

The very last tramcar, no. 616, passes Ansell's brewery, Aston Cross, on its final journey to Erdington. On the motorcycle behind, the pillion passenger is carrying a wreath to mark the end of tram operations in the city. In the distance a Guy Arab IV bus, one of the replacement vehicles for the trams, can be seen coming in the opposite direction.

On the last morning of tram operations car no. 623, on the no. 2 service from Erdington (Chester Road) enters Lichfield Street/Victoria Street junction at the end of her final revenue-earning run, watched by a large crowd. Just beyond this point, passengers will be transferred to waiting buses for the remainder of the journey into the city. Immediately after the Second World War the corporation embarked on an eight-year programme to replace its trams with buses, and many new vehicles were ordered. By 1953 there were sufficient buses to take the trams out of service, although many of the lines had been closed over the previous couple of years. Only the routes to Pype Hayes and Erdington remained open on 4 July. In the months leading up to the closure of the tram system, many enthusiasts' excursions were run as people took the chance to ride the trams for the last time, no doubt putting money into the city's coffers to pay for the new buses that had been ordered or had already come into service.

The very last tram, no. 616, on the no. 2 service, arrives at the Lichfield Street/Victoria Street junction as it completes its final journey, still watched by a large crowd. Many Brummies mourned the passing of the trams, often feeling that they should never have been disposed of so quickly. Indeed, since the late 1960s there have been many proposals brought forward to reintroduce a tram service to the city, culminating in a projected light railway service between Birmingham and Wolverhampton. Other cities, such as Sheffield and Manchester, have reintroduced a tramway system with great success and mainland Europe has never disposed of its tramways. It would appear, therefore, that trams have not been lost forever and their renaissance in Birmingham may not be too far away.

Once the trams had been withdrawn, they were broken up. Sixty such cars were dismantled at Witton depot but the majority were broken up at Kyotts Lake Road works. After being dismantled, the bodies, bogies and so on were removed by lorry to Bird's scrapyard, Stratford-upon-Avon, for final disposal, a very sad end for such a long-lived transport system. Here, at an unidentified location, withdrawn tramcars await their fate after so many years of service.

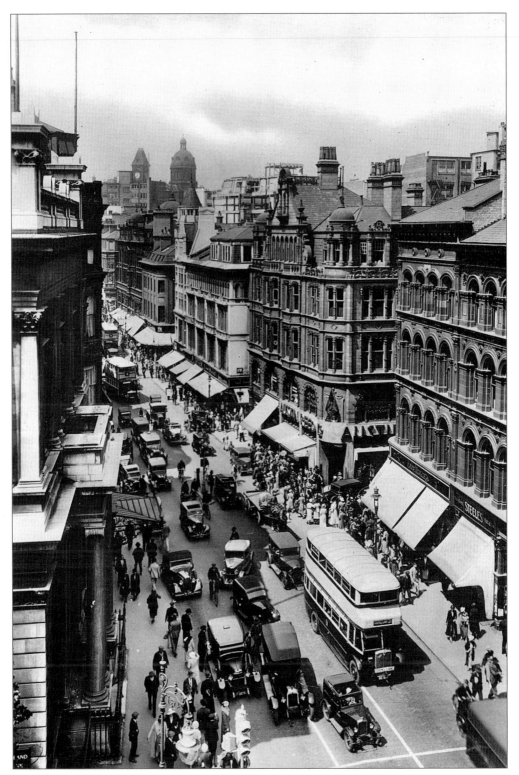

Along with operating its tram network, Birmingham Corporation operated its own bus fleet. In 1904, when the corporation began operating its own public transport system, it inherited a number of Tilling-Stevens' single-deck vehicles and a maintenance works in Tennant Street, near Five Ways from the newly formed Midland Red company. Here, in the 1920s, an AEC Renown double-decker bus, then relatively new, can be seen in Corporation Street.

Corporation Street in the late 1920s with AEC Renown and Regent buses in view, showing several different body styles. There are some pre-First World War buses with open staircases and several buses with enclosed platforms and stairs. Corporation Street was the idea of Joseph Chamberlain (the driving force behind the founding of the University of Birmingham), who envisaged a road similar to the boulevards of Paris. The street was empowered under the Artisans Dwellings Act and building commenced in August 1878; New Street was finally linked with Aston Street in 1903. The cutting of Corporation Street removed some of the worst slums in Birmingham as it progressed.

Daimler COG5 double-decker bus no. 1109 (CVP 209) at King's Heath on 30 August 1952. These buses were very long lived: they were built in 1937 and forty survived until 1960. They were fitted with Gardner 5LW engines and were very reliable. There were also single-deck versions of the COG5 that were replaced by Leyland PS2 buses in 1951. Some of these buses were cut down and used as breakdown vehicles, ensuring that they survived in some form well into the 1970s. I was fortunate enough to gain access to the cab of one of these buses in the 1960s and have liked them ever since.

Although Birmingham bought its share of Leyland, Crossley, Guy and AEC buses, the city has favoured Daimler vehicles since purchasing ten Daimler CP6 double-deckers in 1933. Indeed, of the 2,711 buses purchased before it lost its identity, 2,430 were Daimlers. Birmingham buses were also built to a higher specification than any other municipal bus operator and the body styles were different from those of any other. When, in 1960, Daimler introduced its rear-engined single 'Fleetline' bus it was exhibited in Birmingham Corporation Livery, giving an idea of the influence the city's bus purchases had on the company. The city itself ordered only ten of the new 'Fleetlines' initially, along with eleven of the competitive Leyland 'Atlanteans'. However, the Corporation remained faithful to the Daimler company by making the 'Fleetline' its standard rear-engined vehicle, and went on to order a further 590.

A row of Daimler CV6 double-decker buses at High Street, Deritend, in 1952. The nearest vehicle has the registration number HOV 850 (fleet no. 1850) and its destination board states that it is going to Highgate Road garage. These buses were introduced in 1948 as initial replacements for the trams and were bodied in Birmingham by the Metropolitan-Cammell company. They had the reputation of being the quietest vehicles in the whole of the corporation's fleet. These buses survived until the 1960s, when they were replaced by rear-engined Daimler Fleetline vehicles.

Daimler CV6 bus no. JOJ 2010, one of the last built, is surrounded by 1952-built Daimler CVG6 buses at the Digbeth/Rea Street junction in 1952. These later buses were constructed to replace the trams and were also bodied by Metropolitan-Cammell. Unlike their predecessors their radiators were enclosed. Chassis for these buses were provided by Guy Motors of Wolverhampton and Crossley, as well as Daimler. Production of these later buses continued until 1953, and they survived into the 1970s when they were replaced by more modern Daimler Fleetline vehicles.

A mixture of Daimler CV6 and CVG6 buses on the Digbeth/Rea Street junction in 1952. The rear CV6 is on the no. 54 service to Stechford via Deritend. The Daimler CVG6, JOJ 75 (2075), appears to be heading for the depot. This busy scene also shows an Austin lorry operated by British Road Services, the nationalized haulier created under the 1948 Transport Act, which also nationalized the railways, with an Austin van in the distance. A Bedford lorry can also be seen in this view, along with a Coventry-built Hillman car.

A plethora of buses at the Digbeth/Rea Street junction. There are several Daimler CV6 buses and a couple of Daimler CVG6 buses, one on the 15B route to Garretts Green Lane, South Yardley, and the other on the 44B route to Westley Road. Also in view is the top deck of a Daimler COG5, while in the background are buses belonging to the Birmingham and Midland Motor Omnibus Company (Midland Red).

High Street, Digbeth, in 1953 with a Daimler CV6, registration no. HOV 859 (1859) on the no. 37 route to Hall Green. Also in view is the rear of an AEC Regent Three bus, the corporation owning a few of these, which were mostly based at Acocks Green garage and were used on the Stratford Road services, and a Daimler CVG6 bus. In the background is a Midland Red D4 double-decker bus.

Passing St Martin's-in-the-Bull-Ring church and the 1960s Bull Ring Centre is a Leyland PD2 double-decker. It is about to terminate in the city centre after running a service along the Stratford Road.

CHAPTER FOUR

MIDLAND RED

Just as common a sight on the roads of Birmingham as the primrose and navy blue of the city's buses, Midland Red vehicles operated services that connected the city with other towns in the West Midlands. This had not always been the case, however, as the company, formed on 26 November 1904 as the Birmingham and Midland Motor Omnibus Company, was an amalgamation of several organizations which had operated both motor and horse buses within the Birmingham area.

The name 'Midland Red' was coined before the BMMO actually existed when the Birmingham General Omnibus Company, an amalgamation of several horsebus operators in Birmingham, decided to order new buses in March 1900 and have them painted red. Although this company now had a monopoly on horsebus operations it went bankrupt and its assets were bought from the Official Receiver in January 1902 by the Birmingham and Midland Tramways Ltd, who were themselves taken over by the BMMO on 1 June 1905. At that time the new company took control of fifteen double-deck motor buses which operated over the Hagley Road and Harborne routes. Along with these the company also took control of around 100 horse buses and 1,000 horses. Motor buses obtained by BMMO proved to be unreliable and the company reverted to horsebus operation from 5 October 1907. It was not until 25 May 1912 that BMMO actually began operating motor buses again, these being three Tilling-Stevens petrol-electric vehicles that ran on the Hagley Road and Harborne routes. By this time Birmingham City Tramways was established and it became a condition that no bus services could operate over tram routes, so this was the only route available to BMMO. These vehicles were based at Tennant Street garage, Five Ways, which was transferred to Birmingham City Transport in 1914.

In September 1913 Birmingham Corporation opened a new tram route along the Hagley Road which meant, under 'Watch Committee' rules, BMMO buses could not operate over the route, severely hampering any possibility of them expanding within Birmingham. Thus negotiations were entered into in 1914 that allowed Birmingham Corporation the right to purchase the Tennant Street garage together with thirty Tilling-Stevens double-deck buses while BMMO was not to compete with Birmingham trams, although they could operate buses over tram routes to other towns. Conversely, Birmingham Corporation vehicles would not compete with BMMO outside the city.

After an agreement had been reached BMMO moved its headquarters to Bearwood, near Smethwick, although it maintained garages within Birmingham. In anticipation of the agreement, Midland Red buses began operating with buses from Birmingham to Walsall in 1913 and went on to establish routes all over the Midlands, operating many services from Birmingham. Its Birmingham terminus was at St-Martin's-in-the-Bull-Ring until a new bus station was opened in the new Bull Ring shopping complex during the 1960s. One route from Birmingham to Stratford-upon-Avon was shared with Stratford Blue services, who brought their vehicles into the city. Although there was no rivalry with Birmingham Corporation, Midland Red did have one major competitor, the local railway networks that operated trains to places like Stratford-upon-Avon, Walsall and Evesham.

From 1923 the company designed and built its own vehicles at its Bearwood headquarters, which made it unique, and this practice continued right up until bus deregulation.

In 1969 some of the Midland Red fleet was transferred to WMPTE ownership as Black Country services came under the 1968 Transport Act. These vehicles, mostly BMMO D9 double-deckers, were repainted in WMPTE blue and primrose livery, which certainly did not suit them.

The Midland Red company had its roots in the Birmingham General Omnibus Company (which went bankrupt), whose horse buses trod the streets of Birmingham in the nineteenth century. Here, one of that company's horse buses is seen at Five Ways in the 1890s.

Another of the Birmingham General Company's horse buses seen on the Hagley Road, Edgbaston.

A horse bus arrives outside the General Post Office, New Street, from the Hagley Road at the turn of the century. The post office replaced a temperance hotel that had previously occupied the site. The building was designed by Sir H. Tanner and opened to the public in December 1890, making it a relatively new building when this picture was taken. In the 1960s the post office sought to have the building demolished but opposition from the local Victorian Society forced them to relent, and the old façade has now been incorporated into the new post office building.

Horse power seems to be the order of the day in New Street, which is a street that is far from 'new', dating back as it does to 1553, when Birmingham was referred to as a 'manor'. There are three horse buses in view, the nearest having a destination board for the Hagley Road.

Formed in 1903, the Birmingham Motor Express Company purchased six Milnes-Daimler double-decker buses. In April 1904 a motor bus service from New Street to the Bear Hotel, Bearwood, was introduced. So successful was this service that a route to Harborne was begun in the September of that year. One of the new Milnes-Daimler buses is being inspected in this scene showing the inauguration of the Bearwood route. It was the Birmingham Motor Express Company that formed the BMMO (Midland Red) in November 1904 as a ploy to expand its territory.

The Birmingham Motor Express Company's Milnes-Daimler bus, no. O 266, on the Bearwood service at Hagley Road.

An early Midland Red bus waits outside Birmingham town hall in 1907. The vehicle appears to be a Tilling-Stevens bus. The town hall is pre-Victorian, dating back to the 1830s; it was designed by Messrs Hansom and Welsh and based on the temple of Castor and Pollux in Rome. Building work commenced on 27 April 1832 but things went wrong early on. The architects had underestimated the cost of construction by £8,000, a great deal of money in those days. Also, two men were killed when a pulley block failed. They are buried in St Philip's churchyard, Colmore Row, and a monument was erected in their memory. When the town hall was eventually finished it was 145 feet long, 65 feet wide and 65 feet high. The building was capable of holding about 4,000 people seated or 8,000 standing. The building was first used in October 1834 and was the scene of a riot when David Lloyd George spoke out against the Boer War. The town hall is still in use today, a monument to the town's confidence all those years ago.

An Edwardian view of High Street, Harborne, with the rear view of a horse bus and a Milnes-Daimler motor bus belonging to the newly formed BMMO. By 1911 the Birmingham–Harborne route was the only service available to the Midland Red because of the agreement with Birmingham Corporation that Midland Red would not compete over the tramway system, which was spreading all over the city. At this time the Daimler company was looking to increase its motor bus sales and they approached BMMO with a scheme to provide Birmingham with a fleet of petrol-driven motor buses. Birmingham Corporation were drawn into negotiations but did not possess the necessary powers to operate BMMO services. It would also have taken twelve months for an Act of Parliament to be passed that would allow the city to take over the services so the opportunity was lost. Also, the vehicles suggested by the Daimler company infringed patents held by the Thomas Tilling Company, so the idea foundered. Worse was to follow for the Midland Red. Birmingham Corporation opened a tramway along the Hagley Road on 15 September 1913 which meant that BMMO could not continue its Harborne service. By 1914 agreements were reached so that BMMO was allowed to run through Birmingham to destinations outside it but not compete with the corporation within the city. From this, the Midland Red extended into other areas of the Midlands and operated the services for which it became famous.

Prior to the opening of the bus station as part of the development of the Bull Ring in the 1960s, Midland Red services used the road outside St Martin's church in the Bull Ring as the centre of its Birmingham activities. Here, in about 1927, what appears to be a 1926 SOS FS single-decker bus and a Tilling-Stevens open-top double-decker bus await departure. St Martin's-in-the-Bull-Ring church was a rebuild of a previous structure. It was designed in the gothic style by J.A. Chatwin and was consecrated by the Bishop of Worcester, Dr Henry Philpott, on 20 July 1875.

High Street, Deritend, between Rea Street and Smithfield Street, in 1952, with the steeple of St Martin's church in the background. In view is the yard full of Midland Red buses, including a pair of pre-war SOS FEDD double-decker buses, along with S2 single-decker vehicles and an AEC breakdown vehicle at the back. Following a line of Birmingham Corporation Daimler CV6 buses is an open platformed D2 bus. Midland Red bodied its own buses in this period using fibreglass.

Another view of the Midland Red yard in High Street with SOS FEDD double-deckers and S2 single-deckers in view. Passing by is Birmingham Corporation CVG6 Daimler bus registration no. JOJ 633, fleet no. 2633 on the no. 58 bus service, with an AEC Regent Three ahead. Beyond the AEC, a Midland Red S2 single-decker can be seen heading towards the Bull Ring. Coventry-built Commer lorries and Standard cars can also be seen, along with Oxford-built Morris cars.

Looking along High Street, Deritend, in 1952 and a pair of Midland Red buses are in view. On the no. 159 service is D4 double-decker no. 3780 (registration number NHA 780), while heading in the opposite direction is a D2 double-decker. The D2 is a Brush-bodied AEC Regent Two and was the first of the Midland Red fleet to have a tin front over the radiator. These vehicles were fitted with an AEC 7.58-litre diesel engine, which left them rather underpowered when fully laden. Passing the D4 is a Birmingham City Transport Daimler CVA6 double-decker bus, registration number GOE 597 (1597), introduced in 1947 with a Metropolitan-Cammell body. The corporation bus is operating the no. 37 Hall Green service. The CVA6 buses eventually ended up based at Cotteridge garage and were common on the no. 45 service between Navigation Street and West Heath and the no. 41 service, also from Navigation Street but to Turves Green.

CHAPTER FIVE

PRIVATE TRANSPORT

Although public transport was important to the city, private transport has long been essential to Birmingham's economy, as the city has been the centre for the manufacture of motorcycles and cars. Manufacture of motorcycles in Birmingham came about almost by accident. The BSA company in Golden Hillock Road, Small Heath, as their proper name, Birmingham Small Arms, suggests, were involved in the manufacture of guns in the nineteenth century, a big source of income for Birmingham at that time. However, they decided to produce bicycles during slack periods in the munitions-making process. By the turn of the century they were producing motorcycles and were involved in making Beezer machines for the allied armies during the First World War and continued to do so in the second World War.

From these beginnings other motorcycle manufacturers were established in the city, such as the Ariel company in Selly Oak; Velocette, James and Excelsior in Tyseley; the Sun cycle company of Aston Brook Street; Calthorpe, in Barn Street, and water-cooled Scott's. These companies produced thousands of machines until the 1960s when Japanese competition put them all out of business. Indeed, when I was a teenager, most lads learned to ride on machines such as BSA Bantams or BSA 250cc machines, graduating to BSA 500cc singles, 650cc Gold Star's or Rocket Gold Star's. I recall riding pillion when doing 'the ton' up the Alcester Road, Wythall, on a Rocket Gold Star, an experience I will never forget.

Perhaps the most famous name connected to car production in Birmingham is Austin. When Herbert Austin, a sheep-shearing machine engineer, bought a factory from a wine merchant at Longbridge in 1905, nobody would have believed that the company would become world-famous within twenty years. His first car was exhibited in 1906 and the company produced one new car every two days. So successful was Austin that by 1914 he was employing 2,000 workers. During the First World War the Longbridge works built aircraft for the war effort, a nearby field at Cofton Hackett being used as makeshift landing strip. The Austin works also turned out military vehicles for the army. From that point on, the company went from strength to strength. In the 1950s Austin was merged with Morris Motors of Oxford to form the British Motor Corporation and later mergers brought about the Austin Rover Group (Rover cars being manufactured in nearby Solihull). Nowadays the Austin name has ceased to exist, Rover now being the sole name, but car production still continues at Longbridge despite fears, following the takeover of Rover Group by the German BMW company in 1997, that the Longbridge works might close.

Thus, while motorcycle production has ceased in Birmingham, the manufacture of motor cars still continues and, despite fears to the contrary, the city should see its private transport heritage last into the future.

A production line at the BSA works in Golden Hillock Road, Small Heath, October 1954. It would appear that 500cc single machines are under construction. The little Bantam 125cc motorcycles were also built here, and many a young man graduated to something more powerful after learning to handle one of these bikes. Originally BSA was involved in gun production, and when the First World War broke out they began production of the famous Lewis gun, reaching totals of some 2,000 pieces per week. During the Second World War BSA went back into munitions work and became a target for the Luftwaffe. The factory took a direct hit during the Blitz, with great loss of life. Despite such a setback, however, production of munitions and motorcycles for the armed forces continued virtually uninterrupted. Motorcycle manufacture continued after the war was over and things went well until the Japanese began mass-production of lower-powered motorcycles in the 1960s, which forced BSA, as well as companies such as Velocette and Ariel, out of the small motorcycle market. Ariel did try to hit back with its handsome 200cc Arrow machine but it was too late and most motorcycle production in Birmingham had ceased by the late 1960s. The British motorcycle industry was left with only large and powerful bikes and even these eventually were lost to the Japanese. The BSA finally succumbed to Japanese competition in the early 1970s and the factory was demolished in about 1973: no trace of it now remains. The only surviving record that proves that Birmingham actually produced motorcycles is the collection of Birmingham-built machines displayed at the Birmingham Museum of Science and Industry.

A pre-First World War photograph of Corporation Street, with two motor cars in view; one, registration number OA 1248, appears to be an early Austin. From such small beginnings, the city was to become famous as a centre for motor car construction.

A 1930s view of Ratcliffe Place, close to Chamberlain Square, Birmingham, with a few Austin-built vehicles in view, including an Austin Ruby and an Austin Seven. To the right is the town hall, while on the left is the central library. Designed by E.M. Barry, the library was opened in 1865. It was almost burned down in January 1879 when a workman tried to thaw out frozen pipes with a naked flame. A new fireproof library opened in 1882. This was replaced by the new concrete structure, as part of the inner ring road scheme, in 1971.

An Edwardian view of New Street with an early car close to the Midland Arcade. Also in view is a Milnes-Daimler motor bus of the Birmingham Express Motor Company (later to become part of Midland Red).

A 1908-built 100hp Austin motor car, one of the early vehicles to be turned out of Herbert Austin's Longbridge works.

The car that was to make the Austin Motor Company famous was the little Austin Seven, an example of which is seen here with its owner, Mr William Roberts. This little car was designed in six months by Herbert Austin and his draughtsman, Stanley Edge, and sold for £168. The significance of this smaller model was not initially apparent, the public being used to larger vehicles, and the little Austin was ridiculed until a Cambridge undergraduate announced in *The Times* that he was going to purchase one. This gave the little car 'snob' appeal and it became a great success. This could not have come at a more important time for Herbert Austin, as part of his factory was in the hands of the Official Receiver. From the success of the Austin Seven the Longbridge works became world famous, and would be known for many years as the centre of production for the small car.

Following cessation of hostilities after the Second World War, the Longbridge works geared up to civilian motor car production, after turning out military vehicles and munitions for the war effort. New cars were designed, which included a new 'Baby' car, the Austin A30 and A35, which was introduced in the early 1950s. The design was really a miniature version of the larger A40 Somerset. Here Austin A35 registration number 369 BAU is seen outside Trafford General Hospital, Manchester, in 1997, looking in very good condition some forty years after she was first built.

The same Longbridge-built Austin A35 manufactured in February 1958 and still on the road! Today, she is owned by Sue Clarke-Berry, a nurse who lives in Altrincham, Cheshire. She bought the car in 1996 for £1,700, after it had been restored by an 82-year-old gentleman in Scunthorpe. This A35 is nicknamed Ethel and costs all of £90 a year to insure, fully comprehensive. The car is displayed frequently at classic car rallies and has certainly travelled a long way since her Birmingham birth.

Although Longbridge was known for its small cars, the works also built larger vehicles. Here, in 1963, is one of the Austin production lines assembling A55 Cambridge cars. Shortly after this picture was taken, new Farina-designed A55 and A60 Cambridge cars went into production.

Perhaps the most famous small car of all is the Mini, seen here on the production line in 1963. Designed by Alec Issigonis it was introduced in 1958 and sold for less than £500, even though the car had not been properly costed and made no money for BMC. When the model was first introduced, both the Morris works at Oxford and the Austin works at Longbridge were building these cars. The Oxford-built cars were called Morris Mini Minors (hence the 'Mini' tag) and the Longbridge-produced cars were Austin Sevens, reviving the name of the 1922-designed cars. The Mini quickly became established as a fun saloon, a reputation it retains today, and was helped by successes in rallies and racing. Its image was glamorized further when four of these little cars were used in the feature film *The Italian Job* starring Michael Caine. Despite the best efforts of BMC, British Leyland and the Rover Group to replace the Mini, it still remains in production and has sold over five million vehicles.

Although the Mini has been in production for so long, and many features have changed over the years, the car is still recognizable as the initial production vehicle. Here, a 1987-produced Mini, very much like her predecessors, is seen in Llandudno.

A sporty Mini Cooper of 1997 vintage. The Mini Cooper was first introduced in the 1960s and was phased out a few years later, only to be revamped and reintroduced in the 1990s.

Attempts were made to modernize the appearance of the Mini but Longbridge soon reverted to the original design as the new styling was not popular. Here, an updated vehicle, the Clubman, is on the production line. This particular design did not last very long. It is interesting that, on another production line in the background, the original Mini is still in production – the company appears to be hedging its bets!

Austin Allegros were introduced in the early 1970s and had some novel features including a 'square' steering wheel and 'Hydragas' suspension. I recall these cars being stored at a large yard in Wythall before the launch was announced; the name was taped over, the cars being driven to Wythall straight from the Longbridge production line. At that time the Morris Marina was in production at Oxford and this car appeared to be a smaller version of the Cowley-built car. However, I much preferred the Allegro, and still do. The car was fraught with teething problems after its launch, though, and the square steering wheel was not popular, the company reverting to a more traditional shape in later models. Despite the car's initial unpopularity the Allegro sold reasonably well, and there are still several examples on the road.

A more modern car from the Longbridge production line was the Austin Maestro, seen here in Llandudno. These car
have now been replaced by the new Rover 200 series.

In another attempt to replace the Mini, the Austin Metro was introduced in the late 1970s and named the Mini Metro. At that time the small hatchback car was becoming popular and a special factory to construct these cars was built on land that once carried the old Halesowen branch line through Longbridge. Although a popular car, production of the Metro ceased in 1998 so the Mini still reigns supreme, having beaten off all attempts to replace it. Here, a 1985-built Metro, registration number C327 HGG, is seen in the Austin village at Longbridge. The village was established in 1915 to house the growing influx of munitions workers at the Austin factory. The First World War increased employment at the works from 2,000 in 1914 to a wartime peak of 22,000. In order to house these new employees, Herbert Austin ordered timber houses from the southern USA, half of which were lost when the ship on which they were being transported was sunk by enemy action. These wooden houses still stand and are the subject of a preservation order; residents protested when speculators wanted to buy up the houses to demolish them and replace them with more conventional homes. The atmosphere of this unusual location would almost certainly have been lost.

The Gravelly Hill Interchange, popularly known as Spaghetti Junction, is perhaps the most enduring symbol of Birmingham's importance as a centre of the motor industry.

ACKNOWLEDGEMENTS

I should like to record my thanks to all of those people who have helped put this book together, especially Birmingham Central Library staff, who patiently dealt with my many queries. Others who have helped are Jim Roberts, Arthur Truby, Tim Shuttleworth and Geoff Chapman. I should also like to thank my late wife, Alwen, who was a constant support to me throughout my writing career and often became excited as a new project reached the bookshelves. This support is very much missed.

INDEX